Palgrave Macmillan Memory Studies

Series Editors
Andrew Hoskins
University of Glasgow
Glasgow, UK

John Sutton
Department of Cognitive Science
Macquarie University
Macquarie, Australia

The nascent field of Memory Studies emerges from contemporary trends that include a shift from concern with historical knowledge of events to that of memory, from 'what we know' to 'how we remember it'; changes in generational memory; the rapid advance of technologies of memory; panics over declining powers of memory, which mirror our fascination with the possibilities of memory enhancement; and the development of trauma narratives in reshaping the past. These factors have contributed to an intensification of public discourses on our past over the last thirty years. Technological, political, interpersonal, social and cultural shifts affect what, how and why people and societies remember and forget. This groundbreaking new series tackles questions such as: What is 'memory' under these conditions? What are its prospects, and also the prospects for its interdisciplinary and systematic study? What are the conceptual, theoretical and methodological tools for its investigation and illumination?

More information about this series at
http://www.palgrave.com/gp/series/14682

Margaret Gibson • Clarissa Carden

Living and Dying in a Virtual World

Digital Kinships, Nostalgia, and Mourning in Second Life

palgrave
macmillan

Margaret Gibson
Griffith University
Brisbane, Australia

Clarissa Carden
Griffith University
Brisbane, Australia

Palgrave Macmillan Memory Studies
ISBN 978-3-030-09402-7 ISBN 978-3-319-76099-5 (eBook)
https://doi.org/10.1007/978-3-319-76099-5

Cover credit: Colin Anderson

Printed on acid-free paper

This Palgrave Macmillan imprint is published by the registered company Springer International Publishing AG part of Springer Nature.
The registered company address is: Gewerbestrasse 11, 6330 Cham, Switzerland

A book of this nature is not merely the work of its authors. We owe an enormous debt of gratitude to the residents of Second Life: those we interviewed and those we have met through our fieldwork. This book is for them. We are also grateful to colleagues and particularly to Clare Kennedy who translated into English a small commemorative book written in Italian by a Second Life resident.

Preface

The purpose of this book is to offer an ethnographic analysis of what it means to live, die, and mourn in the virtual world Second Life. Second Life is a valuable space for research as it represents a type of environment that has only now come into being: the mature virtual world. At 14 years old, Second Life can no longer be perceived as the young, cutting-edge environment it once was. As one may expect, it no longer draws swathes of real-world companies to set up headquarters on its shores. In this book we argue that, far from signalling its impending death, these changes mark Second Life's transition to maturity and therefore another kind of significance. Today, Second Life boasts residents who have been involved in their online lives for over a decade. These residents have built homes and communities. They have lived in suburbs. They have been the regular patrons of cafes and bars with friends and family and created and bought virtual objects (e.g. clothing and furniture) that have become imbued with memories and attachments. They've strolled along virtual shorelines hand in hand with lovers and suffered heartbreak. They have patronised art galleries, attended protests, and been the mourners at funerals. In light of these proactive, embedded practices of connection and memory formation with the second lives of others, social death, either by departure while physically alive or departure through actual biological death, has a material and emotional impact. The social departure of Second Life residents, because of biological death, or some other known or unknown reason, creates the need for places and spaces in which to share stories, mourn, and remember. Sometimes second lives go missing, and friends of the missed and missing are not always sure if they are biologically alive, will return to Second Life in the future, or have in fact returned but in another avatar identity and life. This kind of loss and ambiguity creates for those left behind an existential need to find answers and search for the missing or missed, and sometimes decisions are made to pronounce a missing person as dead in their second life. Sometimes this is accompanied by a memorial, which thereby materialises this decision. As it exists today, Second Life is a world with its own culture, its own history, and its own rituals. Much like the offline world, it is a world imbued with memory and mourning.

The book is based on conversations with people who have made lives for themselves in Second Life, including those who have memorialised Second Life and "real-life" friends, lovers, and family members within Second Life. It provokes questions about the value and meaning of a second life and what it means for this life to die, disappear, or become memorialised. For example, are avatars mournable lives beyond the lives and consciousness that animate and give them substance? Can a second life be just as meaningful or even more meaningful than a real life lived in physical space and place? And what can be learned from the stories of lives lived and lost in Second Life memorials and other acts of remembrance? This book asks us to examine what we know or understand about mourning in the realm of virtual world lives and their creative histories.

It is becoming increasingly important in university cultures of teaching to understand how everyday and embedded digital worlds are. This includes an understanding of the everydayness of virtual communities, whether they are social media communities or more place-based communities that include places like Second Life and also social game worlds. University teaching takes place in Second Life, but, in addition to this, university teaching in a more mainstream sense embeds and turns to case studies of our contemporary forms of digital sociality. The growth of books engaged with methodologies of digital ethnographies speaks to the importance of research that not only engages with digital modes of living and digital forms of data collection but also speaks to the reality of social and historical archives as located in the digital. In the last fifteen to twenty years there has been a growing body of research concerned with the place and significance of the digital in practices and processes of memory, mourning, and commemoration. There has been a significant amount of research done on Facebook as a site of digital mourning and commemoration; more recently work is emerging around sites such as YouTube. There is now considerable interest in media cultures and media technologies of mourning (e.g. mobile phones) in which human lives, histories, and memories are created, shared, archived, and lost. These complex, mediated cultures and technologies create macro and micro publics and more private or discrete archives in transnational histories and social networks. We hope that this book will be valuable for researchers in the field of digital ethnography, digital cultures, mourning and memory studies, digital and media sites, and cultures of grief, memorialisation, and nostalgia; and cultural geographers of sites of death, mourning, and memorialisation that work within the sphere of the digital.

Brisbane, Australia

Margaret Gibson
Clarissa Carden

Contents

1 Introduction 1

2 Blended Families 23

3 Grievable Lives 51

4 Commemorative Culture 79

5 Sentimental Objects 107

6 Nostalgia 127

7 Conclusion 145

Index 153

List of Figures

Fig. 1.1	Clara Coates (*left*) and MargieG (*right*) in our preferred avatar forms	14
Fig. 1.2	MargieG (*left*) and Clara Coates (*right*) as "tiny" avatars	15
Fig. 1.3	Clara Coates displaying the "Researcher" tag	16
Fig. 3.1	Clara Coates embodied as an unedited default avatar	55
Fig. 3.2	Editing an avatar in SL	56
Fig. 4.1	MargieG visiting a memorial to the events of September 11, 2001	102
Fig. 5.1	Photograph of Louis's tattoo	115

CHAPTER 1

Introduction

When we enter Second Life (SL) we must always wait for our avatars to load. On a deserted island, at the centre of the city, or on the outskirts of the cemetery, our avatars begin to appear. They load in pieces: sometimes as heads without bodies, sometimes as a series of limbs set at improbable angles. Each time, there is a moment of disconnection: a sense that our avatars, our virtual bodies, may never quite come together. This feeling of fracture, of lag, is part of what it means to be part of SL as an embodied actor through the avatar. At the same time, the vastness of this virtual world can create an orientation of exploration, a sense of being a kind of wanderer. When our avatar bodies come together, as they always do, we can explore spaces which are quite disjunctive, culturally and socially, in terms of their architectures, purpose, and the forms of sociality they offer or expect. We entered into SL through avatar representations with a particular purpose: to try to understand the nature of death, loss, and grief in virtual worlds. In many ways, we started our journey as digital flaneurs, moving through a range of different spaces and cultures within SL to try and glean what they are and might be for their inhabitants. As explorers, wanderers, and flaneurs, however, we found that SL offered a new and disruptive type of experience. It was possible to move from one culture to another with the click of a button. Our exploration required us to be prepared and to have at our disposal many avatar forms, allowing us to follow the rules of engagement wherever we travelled. There is always,

M. Gibson, C. Carden, *Living and Dying in a Virtual World*,
Palgrave Macmillan Memory Studies,
https://doi.org/10.1007/978-3-319-76099-5_1

in SL as elsewhere, a sense of comparative embodiment. It is possible to tell simply by looking at an avatar how invested they are in their identity and in the space they are inhabiting. In order to engage wholeheartedly in SL we had to change our embodiment through shifting avatar forms, enduring the moment of loading, disrupture, and fracture many times in each fieldwork session. These experiences of fracture—fractured bodies and fractured spaces—are strange and confronting to the newcomer. They are, at first, a constant reminder that SL is different to the "real", embodied world one knows and understands. But with time fracture becomes normal, expected. SL itself gains the easy predictability of the "real" world.

Computers and death are uneasy companions. Primed by generations of science fiction novels, movies, and television shows, it is becoming easier to believe that at some point, somehow, the advancement of technology will allow us to shake off that most human of burdens: our mortality. Computers seem to have the most potential to deliver. Companies like Eternime[1] promise to mine our data and create a "digital avatar" through which we can "live forever."[2] Ray Kurzweil, director of engineering at Google, has popularised the idea that a more complete form of uploading—a true transition of the brain to digital form—may be possible within the next few decades. Two episodes of the Netflix programme *Black Mirror* help to illustrate the different forms this digital immortality is purported to take. In *Be Right Back* (2013), a young woman grieving the loss of her partner turns to a digital replica for comfort. Her partner is irrevocably lost, but a computer programme, drawing on data from his emails and social media posts, is able to speak in his voice and express what at first pass for his thoughts. The replica falls far short of the original. *San Junipero* (2016) provides a more optimistic perspective. Here the transfer of the self to the computer is complete—a person can live as a young, embodied self for eternity.

The computer, then, has an important place in popular culture as a technology through which we may one day be able to live forever. This idea speaks to an ideal of the "true self" wherein the self is somehow extricable from the body. The self is in the mind—it is a collection of data which can be uploaded and processed. If the self as mind can be dissociated from the vulnerability of the flesh, then the threat of physical mortality is lessened or removed. In a sense our digital lifestyles lend credence to

[1] "Eternime," n.d., http://eterni.me.

[2] An idea fruitfully examined in Grant Bollmer and Katherine Guinness, "Do You Really Want to Live Forever?," *Cultural Studies Review*, In press.

this notion. We are able to form connections and attachments which appear to exist outside of our physical embodiment. We can present ourselves as we wish—as "true selves," selves of the mind. However, we can never extricate ourselves from the reality of our vulnerable bodies. We remain mortal, and at the moment of death our digital remainders become simply remainders of a life which is no longer.

In this book we use the term "digital flesh" to describe a type of disembodied or differently embodied—but inescapably mortal—form of life. The word "flesh" is rich with associations evoking softness and vulnerability but also ideas of meat—note the similarity to the German *fleisch*—or, in a more abject sense, decomposition. We have chosen the metaphor of flesh over that of the body in order to capture a less discrete figuration of the networked sociality and the co-creative reality of our embodied and storied lives with others. In describing "digital flesh" we recognise the apparent contradiction between mortal, embodied, destructible flesh and clean, data-driven progress as represented by computers. It is in this very contradiction and tension that the term derives its descriptive potency. Members of computer-mediated communities can develop "digital flesh" through ongoing processes of engagement which render them necessarily vulnerable to moral harm. Digital flesh, like embodied flesh, is mortal. However, while every person who enters and engages with a computer-mediated community is mortal, it is not the case that every person will develop digital flesh in this sense. The term implies the development over time of connections, of memories, and of temporal and emotional investments.

In digital modernity human lives are profoundly shaped and intertwined with smart and intelligent machines. This has led to an existential shift in the way relationships are forged, sustained, mobilised, and maintained. Computers, smart phones, Wi-Fi, broadband, fibre optics, apps, and social media, alongside game and virtual worlds, are part of a vast connective tissue of communication and commerce that is central to human life and sociality. Donna Haraway has been a key theorist in understanding the ways in which the human body has merged with machines in a manner that addresses an overlapping between soft flesh and digital flesh. Her concept of the cyborg that involves the interfacing of humans and machines captures the way in which human bodies, psyches, and relationships interact in the virtual spheres of digital life. Human beings have not only "always interacted with technologies,"[3] they are a

[3] Deborah Lupton, "Digital Bodies," in *Routledge Handbook of Physical Cultural Studies*, ed. Michael L. Silk, David L. Andrews, and Holly Thorpe, Routledge International Handbooks (Abingdon, Oxon ; New York, NY: Routledge, 2017).

species characterised by imagination, fantasy, techne, and prostheses. At the same time, we are biological beings, and the sensory and sensuous world of touch and smell grounds our most basic existence and earliest affective bonds. This is transferred and translated, not without difference and loss, into digital lifeworlds. Some digital products and technologies seek more explicitly than others to replicate the intercorporeality of human relationships in circumstances where actual bodily contact is impossible. Apple Watches, a wearable technology which may be connected to the near-ubiquitous iPhone, boast a feature whereby a "digital touch" can be sent from one wearer to another. Using this feature, it is possible to send one's heartbeat to a loved one in another part of the world, who will feel it, through the medium of the watch, on their own wrist.[4]

In the virtual world SL, this type of explicit and physical experiential intercorporeality is impossible. However, the biological anchor of living, breathing, vulnerable bodies serves to connect the digital avatar to the reality of human existence. Without this anchor affective online connections and relationships would be impossible and the grievability of avatar lives unimaginable. In this book we see the relationship between avatar embodiment and the embodied person behind the screen as one of intercorporeality. There is an affective, two-way relationship between these bodies—a critical insight and perspective Tom Boellstorff has brought to ethnography in virtual world environments.[5] As humans we still need to be in touch with the bodies of those we love outside and beyond the digital sphere. But we are also moved and touched by virtual and representational bodies expressed through and embodied in digital code. Unlike Spike Jonze's film *Her* (2013) where a fantasy of intimacy and the development of a relationship take place between a man and his own female-gendered personal operating system, SL is still a world grounded within the human-to-human encounter of the digital screen although the human factor can be morally forgotten because of the avatar and also through the privacy and anonymity that the virtual world SL affords. *Her* is mediated by images of a real-life relationship that failed. As symbolic and psychical wound, the real is displaced by the fantasy of a less complicated relationship and intimacy in the form of a sophisticated technology which is able to replicate, through voice, the presence of a human woman. While the

[4] "Use Digital Touch on Your Apple Watch," Apple Support, accessed November 18, 2017, https://support.apple.com/en-au/HT204833.

[5] Tom Boellstorff, *Coming of Age in Second Life: An Anthropologist Explores the Virtually Human* (Princeton: Princeton University Press, 2008).

absent body is triumphantly discarded, it becomes as the film unfolds a persistent source of loss and longing in memories of the former partner. In our research the avatar is sometimes a tool for maintaining a separation and boundary between real and second life. It is for some a way of conducting relationships, sexual gratification, and experimentation with clear limits and boundaries around real information sharing and emotional investment beyond or through the screen. Residents usually make their boundaries clear in their profile story. However, in the avatar persona in SL, like that of other digital personas in online environments, where identity can be disguised or hidden, hurtful and questionable behaviour is a common problem. A lack of conscience or moral forgetfulness is often called out by residents who will often use the phrase "there are real people behind the avatars." The real is often then a touchstone of morality—a place in which people can be brought back to their moral senses.

In this book we focus on lives constructed and represented through avatars—a means through which the digital flesh becomes embodied as a type of perfected facsimile of living, soft, flesh. Avatar lives and lifeworlds are inevitably intertwined with the consciousness of their flesh and blood creators and animators. However, like characters in a book written by multiple authors in real-time interactions, they quite easily take on life of their own. As a storied life and self, and a digital body, the avatar of a virtual world is not reducible to, or just an extension of, the animator person and body behind the screen. The avatar of SL is largely a textual body, despite appearances, because it is created and sustained socially through conversational processes—written text, read text, and, for some, the addition of the real-life body trace through voice activation. This textual history layers the body of the avatar as its digital flesh providing a particular experience of intimacy and, for many, care and moral responsibility for the life on and beyond the screen, in the unfolding and building of relationships. SL requires a reading of the body that can't be measured against the organic, real-world body as signifying standard even though "in the flesh real world existence" is inevitably where one's sense of human vulnerability and mortality truly resides.

In this book we argue that the death of a person known only online and on screen is a grievable life on its own terms. For the residents of SL who have experienced the death of a dear friend or loved one known only through the medium of the screen, this is not a revelation. Nor is it a revelation for the many residents of other virtual worlds who engage every day in meaningful relationships with others known primarily in their avatar form. However, in light of a lack of recognition of this reality and grievability outside of virtual worlds, it bears repeating. The key defining feature of virtual worlds is that they are technological environments which provide users with a sense of place.[6] Generally definitions of virtual worlds also include the capacity for many people to be online simultaneously and to be able to interact with one another.[7] Virtual worlds share characteristics with massively multiplayer online roleplaying games (MMORPGS) such as World of Warcraft but differ in that they do not possess a storyline or predefined objectives. Arguably, it is possible for a MMORPG to be a virtual world, but it is not necessary for a virtual world to be a MMORPG. Virtual worlds, in part due to their historical and continuing connection to video games, have an uneasy place in public discourse. They are often seen as locations in which issues of addiction or deviancy come to the fore.

Virtual worlds create challenges for ethnographic practices. They are digital, but the boundaries and possibilities of ethnographic exploration in more traditional online media do not necessarily apply. In many cases, online ethnographies are reliant on artefacts.[8] The "place" in which ethnography occurs is a website, a chat board, and a social media platform. The data available comes in the form of text or images—content that in ethnographies of physical communities would be explored in addition to the core subject of analysis. In virtual worlds, what we might call the "placeness" of the physical world is in one sense present. It is possible to observe embodied people interacting, to conduct interviews face-to-face, to emerge oneself in the culture as a visible and participating entity. However, the temporal issues associated with online ethnographic work—the fact that it is not possible to be immersed in one's community of study at all times and the possibility of interruption and thus disengagement from the field as a result of the actions of people around one's physical self—remain a defining aspect of the research process. Virtual worlds have thus been described as blurring online and offline practices of ethnography.[9]

[6] Steven Warburton, "Second Life in Higher Education: Assessing the Potential for and the Barriers to Deploying Virtual Worlds in Learning and Teaching," *British Journal of Educational Technology* 40, no. 3 (May 2009): 416, https://doi.org/10.1111/j.1467-8535.2009.00952.x.

[7] Paul R. Messinger et al., "Virtual Worlds—Past, Present, and Future: New Directions in Social Computing," *Decision Support Systems* 47, no. 3 (June 2009): 204, https://doi.org/10.1016/j.dss.2009.02.014.

[8] Deniz Tunçalp and Patrick L. Lê, "(Re)Locating Boundaries: A Systematic Review of Online Ethnography," *Journal of Organizational Ethnography* 3, no. 1 (April 14, 2014): 65, https://doi.org/10.1108/JOE-11-2012-0048.

[9] Tunçalp and Lê, 67.

However, Boellstorff et al.[10] remind us that the "virtual" as an aspect of human existence far predates the advent of computer cultures. One might consider the "virtual" to be an important aspect of religious and spiritual practices that takes belief outside itself and into connection with some other spiritual entity. Such practices have always been the declared domain of the ethnographer, who cannot access the virtual world entered by the believer but must develop an understanding of it through other means. In computer-based virtual worlds, the ethnographer becomes an active participant. We suggest that the persistence of virtual worlds, both computer-based and rooted in spiritualties, speaks to a very human desire to communicate and form relationships with the "other"—to some entity existing outside everyday spheres of life. The very fact that ethnographers can access and participate in computer-based virtual worlds is demonstrative of the key difference in this new form of relationship—in virtual worlds like SL, the "other" is another person, a fellow traveller with a moral status associated with the inescapable fact of their mortality and vulnerability.

We know, from the work of Boellstorff in particular, that SL is a place.[11] It is a physical environment in its own right, one in which residents—who may in the offline world be on opposite sides of the planet—can be together. Boellstorff's landmark book *Coming of Age in Second Life* was written in the early years of this virtual world's history. At that stage virtual worlds were fresh and exciting. Virtual ethnography was a new genre. Today SL is no longer young. At the time of writing, it is 14 years old. Academics have shown a great deal of interest in this world, particularly in its capacities as a teaching space.[12] At this stage, rather than something

[10] *Ethnography and Virtual Worlds: A Handbook of Method* (Princeton: Princeton University Press, 2012), 22.

[11] Tom Boellstorff, *Coming of Age in Second Life: An Anthropologist Explores the Virtually Human* (Princeton and Oxford: Princeton University Press, 2008); Tom Boellstorff, "For Whom the Ontology Turns: Theorizing the Digital Real," *Current Anthropology* 57, no. 4 (August 2016): 387–407, https://doi.org/10.1086/687362.

[12] Warburton, "Second Life in Higher Education"; Leslie Jarmon et al., "Virtual World Teaching, Experiential Learning, and Assessment: An Interdisciplinary Communication Course in Second Life," *Computers & Education* 53, no. 1 (August 2009): 169–82, https://doi.org/10.1016/j.compedu.2009.01.010; Andrea De Lucia et al., "Development and Evaluation of a Virtual Campus on Second Life: The Case of SecondDMI," *Computers & Education* 52, no. 1 (January 2009): 220–33, https://doi.org/10.1016/j.compedu.2008.08.001; Gilly Salmon, "The Future for (Second) Life and Learning," *British Journal of Educational Technology* 40, no. 3 (May 2009): 526–38, https://doi.org/10.1111/j.1467-8535.2009.00967.x;

fresh and undiscovered, it is a world which has been the subject of sustained academic interest and in which many residents have already lived long, rich lives. It has been part of the daily routine of some residents for over a decade. Technological advances have offered new possibilities for interaction, animation, and building. A recently released update to avatar skeletons, for instance, has allowed more realistic movement, greater adaptability and, for the first time, realistic facial expressions.[13] None of these technological changes have had such an impact on the residents of SL in terms of the way they relate to one another and the way they spend their virtual lives as the duration of their existence in-world.

This book is an ethnographic study of practices relating to grief, memory, nostalgia, and mourning in SL. It contributes not just to research in SL itself but, more broadly and perhaps more importantly, to research relating to a broader transition into digital lifestyles, biographies, and forms of kinship. It aims to rethink digital lives and interrupt some of the conventional media patterns of pathologising screen-mediated relationships. These include the use of the word "addiction" to describe a tendency to engage in virtual worlds for long periods. Psychological discourses and patterns of thinking, which converge around words and terms such as "addiction" and "unhealthy use," serve to problematise engagement with screens and online cultures, particularly where this engagement is carried out by children and young adults. This book presents analyses and narratives that speak to another kind of social imaginary. We seek to construct a counter narrative through which understanding the deeply felt experiences people have in SL is taken for granted as a valuable starting point from which to both conduct research and write about it. In essence, we are using an exploration of something which is itself pathologised, grief, to take on the pathologisation—of online lives. This is a distinctive strategy through which we aim to move beyond the superficial and salacious and to offer a more nuanced understanding of the value of virtual lives. That

Suzanne C. Baker, Ryan K. Wentz, and Madison M. Woods, "Using Virtual Worlds in Education: Second Life® as an Educational Tool," *Teaching of Psychology* 36, no. 1 (January 2009): 59–64, https://doi.org/10.1080/00986280802529079.

[13] "Introducing Project Bento—New Bones Added to Second Life Avatar Skeleton," *SecondLife Community* (blog), December 16, 2015, https://community.secondlife.com/blogs/entry/1855-introducing-project-bento-new-bones-added-to-second-life-avatar-skeleton/; Linden Lab, "Project Bento Live on the Grid!," *SecondLife Community* blog), December 6, 2016, https://community.secondlife.com/blogs/entry/2080-project-bento-live-on-the-grid/.

we do so using ethnography, a practice that has been described as "the opposite of psychological experimentation,"[14] is no accident.

Discourses of addiction relating to internet use have been challenged as failing to take into account the social context in which users engage with online environments.[15] The medicalisation and pathologisation of long-term internet use reduce a complex social phenomenon to an easily understood but ultimately limiting explanation. In SL this discourse is compounded by the presence of the avatar. This, we argue, becomes a kind of site where pathologising discourses are justified and exacerbated. It invokes associations with toys, dolls, or other kinds of gameness. There is also an association with a former generation of video games—one in which the relationship between self and avatar was more limited and relationships with other players were non-existent, fleeting, or rooted in the offline. If one is playing any of an array of older video games—*Sonic the Hedgehog* and *Space Invaders* are key examples—one is moving an object or character on the screen. There is no relationship formation or possibility of connecting with another person. Even if one is embodying a character, it is a character which is preformed. There is also no ability to customise or alter the image which represents oneself in-world. The connection between self and avatar, and between self and other, is shallow or absent. This remnant of other kinds of games and forms of player-avatar relationship contribute to the pathologisation of the avatar and the relationships mediated by avatars. Discursive constructions of such relationships are inflected with these memories. They are also inflected by the potential for constructions of self and other, which are controversial or salacious.

The many possibilities for embodiment offered by the avatar in SL have been at the centre of the often salacious news coverage this virtual world has attracted. In 2007 a paedophilia scandal drew coverage from multiple sources. A sim called Wonderland, set up to look like a playground, was a centre for paedophilic roleplay wherein individuals with the avatar appearance of children met avatars embodied as adult males for sex. First uncovered by Britain's Sky News,[16] it was soon picked up by sources as diverse

[14] Boellstorff et al., *Ethnography and Virtual Worlds*, 38.

[15] Kishonna Gray and Wanju Huang, "More than Addiction: Examining the Role of Anonymity, Endless Narrative, and Socialization in Prolonged Gaming and Instant Messaging Practices," *Journal of Comparative Research in Anthropology and Sociology* 6, no. 1 (2015): 133; Nicola F. Johnson and Helen Keane, "Internet Addiction? Temporality and Life Online in the Networked Society," *Time & Society* 26, no. 3 (November 2017): 267–85, https://doi.org/10.1177/0961463X15577279.

[16] Jason Farrell, "Investigation: Paedophilia And Second Life," News, Sky News, November 4, 2011, https://news.sky.com/story/investigation-paedophilia-and-second-life-10484195.

as Fox News,[17] tech site Engadget,[18] and *The Guardian*.[19] Sex, whether illegal or otherwise, has dominated mass media responses to SL. Stories of couples divorcing due to virtual infidelities[20] or lawsuits over the rights to the code which makes virtual sex possible[21] serve to render SL an apparently deviant space dominated by libido. Now that it is 14 years old, SL attracts less news attention. Where a reporter is assigned to cover a story relating to SL, their copy carries a faint air of astonishment, as though the author believes that this world ought, surely, to have disappeared by now.[22] The fact that it persists goes against the grain of consumer media logic of upgrading, replacing, and letting go of the old for the new. It also speaks to an implicit recognition that the demographics of SL are not "young people" even though the image culture of avatars valorises the appearance of youth.

Despite this disconnection with media logics, SL has in no sense disappeared. Instead, it has been transformed. We argue in this book that SL is now a mature virtual world. It is a world in which residents have lived and lost. It is a world which has seen significant social changes. This is a type of virtual world that has never existed—and which could not exist—at any previous moment in history. This is a book about the maturity that has come with age. Inevitably, as an extension of that, it addresses the memory, loss, and grief that have marked the lives of SL residents. It is also a book about the care and compassion residents show towards one another and about the strength of the attachments that are formed online.

[17] Associated Press, "Paedophile Playground Discovered in 'Second Life' Virtual World," News, Fox News, November 2, 2007, http://www.foxnews.com/story/2007/11/02/pedophile-playground-discovered-in-second-life-virtual-world.html.

[18] William Dobson, "Second Life 'Wonderland' scandal Hits Mainstream Media," Engadget, October 31, 2007, https://www.engadget.com/2007/10/31/second-life-wonderland-scandal-hits-mainstream-media/.

[19] Kate Connolly, "Second Life in Virtual Child Sex Scandal," *The Guardian*, May 9, 2007, sec. Technology, http://www.theguardian.com/technology/2007/may/09/secondlife.web20.

[20] William Lee Adams, "UK Couple to Divorce over Affair on Second Life," *Time*, November 14, 2008, http://content.time.com/time/world/article/0,8599,1859231,00.html.

[21] Phil Davis and Associated Press, "'Second Life' Avatar Sued over Virtual Sex Device," ABC News, August 16, 2007, http://abcnews.go.com/Technology/story?id=3468709&page=1.

[22] E.g. "Why Is 'Second Life' Still a Thing?," Motherboard, accessed July 7, 2017, https://motherboard.vice.com/en_us/article/z43mwj/why-is-second-life-still-a-thing-gaming-virtual-reality; Rachel Metz, "Remember Second Life? Its Creators Are Back with a Virtual Reality Platform," MIT Technology Review, January 27, 2017, https://www.technologyreview.com/s/603422/second-life-is-back-for-a-third-life-this-time-in-virtual-reality/.

In this book we aim to denaturalise and interrogate the ontological categories of firstness and secondness that are built into Second Life's very name. While many residents retain this distinction and position themselves as having a moral commitment to privilege first life over second life, this does not negate the families and everyday forms of connection that exist primarily or only in SL but nonetheless demand their time. This leads to tensions between the ways in which these categories of firstness and secondness are mobilised. These categories become more complex where residents spend significant time in SL. Time spent online has intrinsic value. The time one spends in SL becomes an investment in one's own virtual life and the relationships one forms through the screen. It is a finite resource that one has, for whatever reason, poured into life in the virtual world rather than some other forms of life. For some residents, over time, meeting offline and encountering loved ones in a physically embodied form loses its value as the ultimate or only touchstone through which a relationship is defined as real or valuable. As such, firstness and secondness do not always function as adequate explanatory categories for understanding hierarchies of relationships formed by SL users. As Garcia et al. argue, the "virtual world" is not a distinct reality somehow outside other social spheres.[23] It is part of a broader social world, a place with its own rules of engagement but which ought not to be immediately defined as less important than other places simply because of its virtualness. Residents may think of their virtual lives as secondary in relation to their lives offline, but these boundaries can and do break down.

Virtual worlds displace the conventional rules of engagement relating to family and romantic relationships. They are not governed by the same everyday normativities and moralities as the world offline. Within these environments it becomes possible to contest legal and social norms of care and relatedness. However, these contestations are often only possible or valued within SL itself. Doka's theory of disenfranchised grief provides an important conceptual tool with which to understand the grieving experiences of SL residents who lose beloved friends, family, and indeed places. Disenfranchised grief occurs where a loss is not socially recognised and cannot be publically mourned. A person experiencing disenfranchised grief does not have a right to grieve "since no one else recognises a legitimate cause of grief."[24] There is a range of situations in which this can

[23] Angela Cora Garcia et al., "Ethnographic Approaches to the Internet and Computer-Mediated Communication," *Journal of Contemporary Ethnography* 38, no. 1 (February 2009): 54, https://doi.org/10.1177/0891241607310839.

[24] Kenneth J Doka, "Disenfranchised Grief," in *Living with Grief: Loss in Later Life*, ed. Kenneth J Doka (Washington, DC: The Hospice Foundaion of America, 2002), 160.

occur. The most relevant to our context is when a relationship is not recognised or a loss is not acknowledged.[25] One category of grief routinely disenfranchised is that which follows ambiguous loss—the grief that occurs where no one has died or where it is uncertain that a person has died.[26] Another is the grief of a person who is not a family member.[27] These issues of ambiguity and proximity have a special relevance in a context where residents may grieve the loss of people whom they have not met offline.

Attig argues that the word "disenfranchise" wrongly implies that the denial of the right to grieve is the denial of an entitlement that institutions are able to grant. Instead, he describes the right to grieve as a matter of human dignity "grounded in recognition of the nature of human attachments and the inherent needs and desires of all who live in the human condition to grieve in their own ways when loved ones die."[28] Attig states that disenfranchisement compounds suffering and, by failing to deal meaningfully with suffering, fails to support a return to thriving.

Kamerman states that if disenfranchised grievers were allowed to express their grief with the same legitimacy as currently enfranchised grievers, it may serve to legitimate the nontraditional relationships that lead to disenfranchisement.[29] However, he indicates that this may also undermine and complicate the grief of currently enfranchised grievers, undermining the support that is provided by legitimacy. He provides the example of a wife's emotions if a mistress is able to attend her husband's funeral and post an obituary.[30] In many cases offline family members have been unaware of the rituals which were enacted by SL loved ones. In those instances where a relative of the deceased has become aware, our research has shown that they have embraced the commemoration of their loved one's lives by their online friends. For those residents who grieve the loss of those they have only encountered within SL, the ability to have this grief recognised outside of the boundaries of that world is limited. Many of the practices we describe are acts of recognition and rejection of the disenfranchisement of grief. Residents construct and enact their own rituals that

[25] Doka, 160.

[26] Pauline Boss and Janet R Yeats, "Ambiguous Loss: A Complicated Type of Grief When Loved Ones Disappear," *Bereavement Care* 33, no. 2 (May 4, 2014): 65–66, https://doi.org/10.1080/02682621.2014.933573.

[27] Doka, "Disenfranchised Grief," 161.

[28] "Disenfranchised Grief Revisited: Discounting Hope and Love," *OMEGA—Journal of Death and Dying* 49, no. 3 (2004): 198.

[29] "Latent Functions of Enfranchising the Disenfranchised Griever," *Death Studies* 17, no. 3 (May 1993): 284, https://doi.org/10.1080/07481189308252624.

[30] 286.

highlight the fact that their relationships, their lives, and their losses are real and demand commemoration.

These losses occur in a world predominantly based on the creative possibilities it offers. The official website for SL lists a range of areas one might choose to explore. It features sections on creativity, entertainment, social opportunities, real estate, education, and business.[31] The slick, modern site targets users from a range of occupations and with an array of goals. Potential residents are told that they can "[s]tart a business & earn real profits" or "[d]iscover incredible experiences, fascinating people, and vibrant communities."[32] As a landing page, it says very little about the virtual world itself, and indeed it is difficult to ascertain from this bland, corporate visage precisely what SL has to offer.

Dig a little deeper on this website, and the true diversity—and potential—of SL begins to be evident. A list of accepted payment methods for the 50 most active countries reveals that SL residents hail not only from English-speaking countries (e.g. USA, UK, Canada, Australia) but from throughout Europe (e.g. Belgium, Denmark, Finland), Latin America, (e.g. Mexico, Puerto Rico), Asia (e.g. China, Japan, South Korea), and the Middle East (e.g. Israel, Turkey), alongside other nations such as Russia and Ukraine.[33] It is clear, therefore, that SL is transnational and potentially even global. It is open to participants from many language groups and geographical locations. While the impact of this should not be overstated—it remains the case that the de facto language of SL is English—prolonged engagement with SL almost necessitates intercultural interaction and encounters with translation and digital translation tools. This sort of intercultural engagement has been shown to occur in various locales, including those where it was not expected, such as science fiction discussions and poetry readings.[34]

Our engagement in this virtual world has occurred through the medium of the avatar. Our avatars, MargieG and Clara Coates, are our physical

[31] Linden Labs, "Official Site | Second Life—Virtual Worlds, Virtual Reality, VR, Avatars, Free 3D Chat," accessed July 31, 2017, http://secondlife.com/.

[32] Linden Labs.

[33] Linden Labs, "List of Accepted Payment Methods by Country," SecondLife Community, accessed July 31, 2017, https://community.secondlife.com/knowledgebase/english/list-of-accepted-payment-methods-by-country-r1396/.

[34] William C. Diehl and Esther Prins, "Unintended Outcomes in Second Life : Intercultural Literacy and Cultural Identity in a Virtual World," *Language and Intercultural Communication* 8, no. 2 (May 2008): 111, https://doi.org/10.1080/14708470802139619.

Fig. 1.1 Clara Coates (*left*) and MargieG (*right*) in our preferred avatar forms

representation in-world and the face we present to informants, friends, and strangers alike (Fig. 1.1). The avatar is a key mode of presenting information about oneself in-world. This importance has been noted in existing research: for instance, physical aspects of the avatar have been shown to be a more reliable indicator of age than linguistic features of resident dialogue. One study in SL found that older residents are more likely to use avatars that are female, shorter, and gender idealised, whereas younger residents are more likely to use alternative avatars, including furries.[35]

Avatars are almost infinitely customisable and therefore tell a great deal about the person using them. They are also susceptible to moral or ethical harm. Vanacker and Heider state that where a person identifies strongly with their avatar, they are particularly likely to be harmed by actions that violate that avatar.[36] Avatars can be an important aspect of a person's identity, they note, and relationships engaged in by avatars can be intensely

[35] Rosa Mikeal Martey et al., "Communicating Age in Second Life: The Contributions of Textual and Visual Factors," *New Media & Society* 17, no. 1 (January 2015): 41–61, https://doi.org/10.1177/1461444813504270.

[36] B. Vanacker and D. Heider, "Ethical Harm in Virtual Communities," *Convergence: The International Journal of Research into New Media Technologies* 18, no. 1 (February 1, 2012): 71–84, https://doi.org/10.1177/1354856511419916.

meaningful.[37] The potential for meaningful relationships to exist between avatars has been recognised by professionals, for instance, by counsellors who work in SL.[38]

Our avatars also speak to our level of technical competency—however limited—and our willingness to engage fully with the groups in which we find ourselves. We each have a form which has become our default. For MargieG (Margaret), this is a blonde Caucasian woman wearing a dress jacket and pants. For Clara Coates (Clarissa), it is a very pale Caucasian woman with dark hair wearing a dark dress. However, our fieldwork has seen us take on several forms. Most of these have been human. We have experimented with changes of hairstyle, makeup, and clothing. Some of this has been for fun. At times, however, we have altered our avatars specifically to gain entry to particular locations. We each have a few 1920s style outfits for use when visiting 1920s Berlin (discussed in a later chapter). We also both have a "tiny" avatar—a small, cute, cartoonish animal form. MargieG is a husky, while Clara Coates is a red squirrel with a range of doll-like costumes (Fig. 1.2). Neither of us has ever used a male avatar,

Fig. 1.2 MargieG (*left*) and Clara Coates (*right*) as "tiny" avatars

[37] Vanacker and Heider, 77.

[38] Karl J. Witt, Marvarene Oliver, and Christine McNichols, "Counseling via Avatar: Professional Practice in Virtual Worlds," *International Journal for the Advancement of Counselling* 38, no. 3 (September 2016): 218–36, https://doi.org/10.1007/s10447-016-9269-4.

although there is nothing that prohibits us from doing so. On the whole, our preferred avatars look like idealised versions of ourselves.

We have clearly identified ourselves as researchers at all times during our fieldwork. In SL, it is possible to form groups. A resident can have one group active at a time, and the resident's title in that active group will appear above their head. We formed a group called "Margaret and Clarissa research" and chose the tag "Researcher" (see Fig. 1.3). Anyone with their Second Life Viewer set to display the names and tags of other residents would have been aware of our position. Further, our position as researchers was identified in our user profiles, and we provided potential interviewees with links to our university staff pages.

The stories we explore in these pages have been generously shared by some of the residents who call SL home. For many, these stories have been deeply personal, speaking to painful losses and intimate relationships. In order to protect the identities of our interviewees, we have used pseudonyms. The only cases where this has not occurred are those where a story of person is particularly well-known and cannot be discussed without a reader familiar with SL being able to ascertain their identity. These residents are SL celebrities—we acknowledge their public role and write sensitively about their lives and works. Boellstorff et al, in *Ethnography and Virtual Worlds*, note that researchers approaching virtual worlds will often

Fig. 1.3 Clara Coates displaying the "Researcher" tag

find that there is no clearly delineated community as such.[39] There is always an element of choice in defining the boundaries of ethnographic study in such an environment. Who and what one studies will necessarily influence the method of study. Our focus has been on death and memory. Our research has therefore centred around spaces such as cemeteries, memorials, and historical sites. This does not mean that we have not interacted with residents outside these sites: indeed, we have welcomed any opportunity to be introduced to new communities and residents with different experiences. However, the focus of our research has determined who we have interviewed and the spaces we have frequented.

Driscoll and Gregg highlight the importance of acknowledging one's own position and relationship to the online environment in conducting an online ethnography.[40] As researchers, we bring very different backgrounds to our ethnographic exploration. Margaret is an academic with a research background in death, grief, and memory. She has been in SL since November 2011, having made an account in order to carry out research. On her initial entry to SL, she felt very much the outsider. She was unfamiliar with the mechanics of either virtual worlds or video games. Margaret's difficulty in controlling her avatar was reflected in MargieG's actions online. MargieG occasionally stepped on graves or performed other transgressive actions as a result of the inexperience of her operator. Over six years, Margaret has become more competent and comfortable in the virtual world. She is able to perform actions like dressing her avatar and moving in crowded areas without difficulty. Her growing confidence in the SL platform has corresponded with a growing sense of connection to her avatar, MargieG. She no longer describes MargieG as "my avatar" but as "me." However, she still feels that there is a level of effort required in operating SL. She is constantly aware that she is not a digital native and that existing within a virtual environment is a constant learning process.

Clarissa has played many roleplaying games on computers and game consoles. She did not experience the sense of disconnection between self and avatar that characterised Margaret's early SL experience, nor did she find the SL interface difficult to use. Clarissa joined the project in early 2016. While she made a new SL account to do so, this was not her first foray into the virtual world. In 2006–2007, aged 15–16, she had spent

[39] *Ethnography and Virtual Worlds*, 57.

[40] "My Profile: The Ethics of Virtual Ethnography," *Emotion, Space and Society* 3, no. 1 (May 2010): 15–20, https://doi.org/10.1016/j.emospa.2010.01.012.

time in SL with offline friends. As teenagers, none had access to the credit card required to purchase land or hold a premium account. She was therefore a homeless resident, enjoying building and exploring but unable to set up her own residence or engage meaningfully with SL's extensive shopping culture. Her strongest memory of this time—and the aspect of SL that made her choose to leave—was of sexual harassment by residents with male avatars. This occurred primarily in places frequented by new residents such as large emporiums offering free items. Harassment would even extend to tricking women to travel to sexually suggestive locations and to use poseballs which would place their avatars in compromising positions. This aspect of SL has not changed. On her first entrance to SL as Clara Coates, she was taken to a beach by a resident using a masculine avatar and asked to use a poseball. She immediately teleported home. One of her friends from university, upon entering SL for the first time, promptly found herself teleported into a sex dungeon, logged out, and never signed in again.

These early experiences suggest that some aspects of SL are confusing, intimidating, and exploitative. These have been mediated by the outward femininity of our avatars. Once we became integrated into SL, however, we discovered a world populated by extraordinarily kind, generous people. Our very newness on entry to SL led to strangers attempting to help us navigate our new world. As we became more accustomed to the space—and to the ordinary tasks of changing clothes, decorating our homes, and indeed moving our avatars in this three-dimensional environment—we were able to interact on a more equal footing with experienced residents.

Time has been a key issue for us as researchers. Working from Australia, we have been out of step with SL time, which is based on the time in San Francisco where Linden Lab is located. While it is possible to conceive of time online in terms of "cybertime," the time used by the digital city, this does not mitigate the real issues inherent in attempting to interact in real time with a person living in a different time zone. The digital day is therefore a day that is retemporised in relation to the offline day.[41] For us this meant that if we wanted to be present in SL early on Sunday morning, we had to be online shortly after midnight on Monday. As working academics and mothers, we found that the temporality of SL did not fit neatly around our commitments to teaching, parenting, and other research. It required a shift in our understanding of what constituted our working day and a need to become aware of the time of day in a very different part of the

[41] Michel Laguerre, "Virtual Time," *Information, Communication & Society* 7, no. 2 (January 2004): 223–47, https://doi.org/10.1080/1369118042000232666.

world. Our experience demonstrates that the way in which one's life in SL is scheduled around one's commitments offline is highly influenced by geographical location. While SL is indeed a world of its own, it is a world one must access from a time and place outside its boundaries.

Themes of the Book

The remainder of this book explores five important themes that, together, provide a picture of the many and complex ways in which people live, die, and grieve in SL. In Chap. 1 we examine families in SL: the ways in which they are formed, their purpose, and the way in which they are grieved. These families alternatively undermine and reinforce traditional forms of kinship. These families can be combinations of "real-life" biological kinship (mothers, daughters, sisters, aunts—female kinship networks predominate) with "adopted" digital kinships of SL children (sons, daughters, fathers, mothers, sisters, brothers) and partners. While sexuality in SL has attracted much media attention, the deeper, longer-lasting, and more significant family relationships that are made possible within this environment have received less notice. Our aim, in bringing the blended families of SL to the fore, is to undermine narratives which hold that SL relationships are primarily sexual or indeed that they are shallow and false. However, we also acknowledge the different levels of engagement and commitment to family life experienced by residents.

The construction of families and significant relationships within SL highlights the potential for meaningful connection through the medium of the avatar. In Chap. 2 we argue that lives lived in SL—avatar lives—are themselves meaningful and grievable even as separate from the embodied life required for their operation. Second lives are dependent upon physical existence; however, in keeping with our commitment to problematise notions of firstness and secondness, we argue that a second life is not reducible to an extension of a "real life" (RL). Avatars themselves develop extensive networks of relationships, amass property, and create items that have economic value both within and outside the virtual world. They can hold positions of responsibility and trust within their virtual communities. These are aspects of lives that, we argue, are real, fulfilling, and grievable. This chapter considers this possibility in relation to the illness, disability, and loss that are disproportionately present in the accounts of SL residents interviewed by the authors. We consider whether physical limitations outside the virtual world have an impact on the development and grievability of virtual lives.

The first two chapters establish the connectedness and autonomy of second lives, demonstrating that avatar lives are distinct from physical lives and have value as part of their own networks of friends and family. In the third chapter, we show the way in which the commemorative culture of SL materialises the grievability of second lives as semi-autonomous as well as the grievability of more blended lives. In this chapter we consider the culture around commemorating and remembering important people and events. We describe the phenomenon of SL cemeteries in which people and animals, both existing within and outside the virtual world, are memorialised. We also explore public memorials that serve as sites of memory for people and events outside the SL context.

While the previous chapters contained stories of grieving and grievability based on interviews and conversations, this chapter will focus on the spatial geographies of grief through commemorative sites that include and blend real news events of celebrities, disasters, and wars with the personal grief of SL residents. This chapter engages in the politics of grievability through SL's extensive and diverse commemorative culture. This politics unsurprisingly extends and produces (not simply reproduces) hierarchies of grief in a global and often nationalist context. This becomes an important recognition of the kind of potential neocolonialism and imperialism of US-centric emotionalism around the grievability and value of American lives as they become situated in avatar and virtual-world cultures. Some commemorative spaces are more living than others in terms of continuing visitation. This chapter will explore the material practices around who or what is grievable through monuments, memorial sites, special days of remembrance, and cemeteries.

We then return to the personal and, in Chap. 4, consider the more personalised and domestic material culture of grievability in SL. The nearly unlimited ability to create objects is one of Second Life's most appealing and well-publicised features. It is at the heart of what Boellstorff describes as creationist capitalism.[42] In this chapter we discuss those objects to which SL residents have a sentimental attachment. We discuss the way in which objects can serve as reminders of loved ones who have either died or moved on. We also discuss the way in which SL residents consciously replicate and reproduce meaningful objects they encounter outside SL such as items relating to home, clothing, and even pets. Finally, we consider the fate of objects whose owners have "died"—either virtually, through ceasing to

[42] Boellstorff, *Coming of Age in Second Life*.

enter the virtual world or through the physical death of the person behind the avatar.

In Chap. 5 we engage with notions of memory and nostalgia as they emerge in SL. The first section of this chapter deals with nostalgia for home. This section is based on interviews with two women from very different class backgrounds who constructed, with the resources available to them, significant spaces of memory for their elderly mothers. We link this discussion about nostalgia for real-life histories, lost or imagined, in the digital, with an analysis of manifestations of nostalgia for SL's own history within the virtual world. These manifestations include important spaces from previous iterations of the world, preserved despite developments in building practices rendering them outdated, which are available for the public to visit. They also include museums and exhibitions dedicated to SL's history. Finally, we conclude the chapter by discussing the notion of time travel as it is manifested in SL. We consider the case of the 1920s Berlin Project, a popular simulation aiming to replicate as closely as possible the appearance and conditions of Berlin during the 1920s. We also consider other historical simulations and their connection to more personal acts of nostalgia within the virtual world.

This book provides the most complete study of death, grief, and memory in SL to date. However, its significance goes beyond this specific virtual world. This is a book that speaks to the experiences of individuals living, forming connections, and grieving in a mature virtual world, a new type of entity not possible at any other point in history. As such, it is an important contribution to our understanding of digital lifestyles and the way in which practices relating to loss are adapted to and carried out within digital environments. The lives in SL are, we argue, problematised by the presence and potential meanings of the avatar. The avatar provides an embodied self which, given the near-infinite possibilities offered by SL, can carry out the motions of mourning which would be familiar were they enacted by a physically embodied self. The avatar thus creates an appearance of simulation open to interpretation as something unhealthy or false in a way that is not necessarily possible in relation to other forms of online grieving. However, the avatar is also central to the development of the very lives and relationships that are grieved and grievable.

In writing this book, we begin by taking for granted the fact that it is possible to feel experiences deeply through the medium of the avatar and that emotions associated with people known only through the avatar are real and valid. In doing so, we hope to upend notions of the avatar as a type of false embodiment which hides the "real self" of the user. Instead, we recognise communication between avatars as simply a mode of communication and places inhabited by avatars as simply places. This position allows us to explore our subject outside the pathologising lens offered by psychological discourses and to instead recognise SL cultures as cultures with valid practices worthy of study.

CHAPTER 2

Blended Families

Introduction

The concept of "digital kinship" captures how doing and being a family, along with constructions of relatedness itself, is increasingly, if not overwhelmingly, embedded within networked environments.[1] In a mediatised world, kinship as Hjorth et al. write, "moves in and out of online and offline spaces" which in turn "have come to develop their own histories, connections and memories."[2] The authors suggest that, rather than viewing family interactions as occurring either online or offline, it is more useful to consider the forms of "intimate co-presence"[3] through which relationships are maintained. While Hjorth et al. focus on families who are recognised offline as having "real" familial relationships, the term can be usefully extended to recognise the types of digital kinships which can form online.

There is nothing inherently surprising about relationships, particularly romantic relationships, emerging online. Indeed, thanks to the rise of apps such as Tinder, and the continuing presence of older dating websites such

[1] Larissa Hjorth et al., "Digital Kinships: Intergenerational Locative Media in Tokyo, Shanghai and Melbourne," in *The Routledge Handbook of New Media in Asia*, ed. Larissa Hjorth and Olivia Khoo (London ; New York: Routledge, Taylor & Francis Group, 2016), 251–61.

[2] Hjorth et al.

[3] Hjorth et al., 252.

M. Gibson, C. Carden, *Living and Dying in a Virtual World*,
Palgrave Macmillan Memory Studies,
https://doi.org/10.1007/978-3-319-76099-5_2

as OkCupid, the stigma has largely been removed from romantic attachments that emerge in digital environments and connectivities. Dating apps and the internet now occupy that mythic locus of the origin from which stories about how relationships and friendships came into existence are told and shared. The avatar, however, brings a new dimension to the way in which this is understood and socially visualised. It has the potential to be viewed as a form of masking and a particularly false face through which true connection cannot be established. Even if connections originating online are the "new normal," then relationships mediated by avatars nonetheless remain "abnormal."

The hyper-gendered normativity of much avatar physicality, and the opportunities available for experimentation and sexual exploration, has led to popular and academic interest in the romantic attachments and sexuality of SL residents.[4] Less attention has been paid to the more complex family configurations which are constructed and maintained by residents. It is not uncommon for SL residents to form networks of kinship in-world. SL families may include a variety of relationships: from people who are relatives or close friends in RL to loved ones who are known only in SL to families including some mixture of both. Some families include members which are not residents at all but animated objects such as the popular prim babies. The inclusion of such objects—which can also take the form of a beloved prim pet—speaks to another form of blending. This is the blending of people represented by their avatars with something akin to an avatar which exists without a human operator (although of course humans designed and programmed such objects). In SL residents may adopt someone as a sibling, an aunt, a parent, a child, or a partner. Such relationships may be formed organically or through more formal means. A range of adoption agencies catering to different family structures exist in-world. These agencies connect residents who wish to form parent-child relationships. Our first introduction to blended families within SL came with the discovery of family plots.[5] These plots provide spaces for multiple members

[4] Anastasia Slater, "Virtually Yours: Desire and Fulfillment in Virtual Worlds," *The Journal of Popular Culture* 44, no. 5 (2011): 1120–37; Ashley John Craft, "Love 2.0: A Quantitative Exploration of Sex and Relationships in the Virtual World Second Life," *Archives of Sexual Behavior* 41, no. 4 (August 2012): 939–47, https://doi.org/10.1007/s10508-012-9933-7.

[5] As discussed in Margaret Gibson, "Grievable Lives: Avatars, Memorials, and Family 'Plots' in Second Life," *Mortality* 22 (January 12, 2017): 224–39, https://doi.org/10.1080/13576275.2016.1263941.

of the same SL family, whether or not they are members of the same RL family, to be memorialised together. Our understanding of blended families has therefore been shaped by an awareness of the loss and grief associated with the closure or irreparable alteration of these relationships through death.

In this chapter we discuss both "blended families" and "chosen families," the latter being a term coined by Kath Weston to describe the intimate networks of close friends cultivated by gay and lesbian people who may otherwise have limited family ties.[6] This phenomenon has been identified even in nations which are broadly supportive of gay and lesbian people.[7] We use the term "chosen families" to denote family configurations in which all members are family only through their own decision to describe themselves in this way and "blended families" to denote family groupings including persons who are related, legally or through blood, offline. Both types of family arrangement may be usefully understood within the broader framework of digital kinships. This differentiation is complicated by the fact that some SL chosen family relationships do indeed extend offline and can be recognised by participants as equal to legal or biological family relationships. One interviewee, Edmund, said of his SL brother, Sam, that:

> I didn't realise, actually, until his funeral that it extended past SL and into RL. He had his biological brother, who he didn't get along with, and his adopted sister and me, and when I found out about that, it rather destroyed me. I had to excuse myself to go bawl outside.

Edmund's relationship with Sam was unusual in that they were able to meet offline and that their connection to one another as chosen siblings was recognised by friends and family to the extent that Edmund and his RL partner were able to attend Sam's funeral. Despite this, it was only after the moment when the potential for new interactions within this relationship was destroyed by Sam's death that Edmund was able to comprehend the true significance of the relationship. Edmund gained a deeper intimacy with his brother and potentially a greater right to grieve his loss at this moment of realisation, during the funeral itself. This added to his

[6] *Families We Choose: Lesbians, Gays, Kinship*, Between Men—between Women (New York: Columbia University Press, 1997).

[7] Alexis Dewaele et al., "Families of Choice? Exploring the Supportive Networks of Lesbians, Gay Men, and Bisexuals," *Journal of Applied Social Psychology* 41, no. 2 (2011): 312–31.

grief in that he was not able to discuss this altered relationship with his brother. The relationship, now even more significant than before, was lost. There was no potential to construct new memories, but those that remained were made more precious.

Doka writes that societies establish roles about who has a legitimate right to grieve, with these rights corresponding to forms of primarily family relationship. Such rules do not necessarily correspond to the strength or nature of a particular attachment. This can occur in a range of situations such as where the relationship between the deceased and the grieving person is not recognised, where the loss itself is not recognised, where the loss itself is disenfranchising, or where the griever is not recognised (e.g. because they are very young or intellectually disabled).[8] This leads to a paradox in that the nature of disenfranchised grief can itself exacerbate grief. It can also require grief to remain private and cut the bereaved off from social support and from the rituals associated with death.[9]

Where a loving relationship is not socially recognised or not recognised in the majority of spaces in which an individual lives, their life there is a serious risk that, upon the death of one party, the survivor experiences disenfranchised grief. For example, the grief of gay and lesbian bereaved partners, particularly in older couples, has been shown to be disenfranchised for a range of reasons including where one or both members of the couple have not "come out" to their families.[10] Hensley notes that, due to the relatively low level of public engagement with virtual worlds like SL, people who are heavily involved in such communities spend their daily lives surrounded by people who do not understand virtual worlds. As a result they are at a high risk of experiencing disenfranchisement of their grief if they suffer loss online.[11] She conducted a study of people who had lost a friend or loved one in any of a range of virtual worlds. She found that some respondents characterised their relationship with the deceased

[8] Kenneth J Doka, "Disenfranchised Grief," *Bereavement Care* 18, no. 3 (December 1999): 37–38, https://doi.org/10.1080/02682629908657467.

[9] Doka, 39.

[10] Bryan McNutt and Oksana Yakushko, "Disenfranchised Grief Among Lesbian and Gay Bereaved Individuals," *Journal of LGBT Issues in Counseling* 7, no. 1 (January 2013): 87–116, https://doi.org/10.1080/15538605.2013.758345.

[11] Lisa D Hensley, "Bereavement in Online Communities: Sources of and Support for Disenfranchised Grief," in *Dying, Death, and Grief in an Online Universe: For Counselors and Educators*, ed. Carla Sofka, Illene Noppe Cupit, and Kathleen R. Gilbert (New York: Springer Pub, 2012), 121.

as very close but did not feel able to grieve publicly. They also did not feel that they had a right to connect with the in-person loved ones of the deceased.[12]

The barrier between the "real" and the "virtual" therefore serves to determine the way in which losses are grieved. The distinction between the "real" and the "virtual" has been challenged by Boellstorff[13] and is a distinction we also hope to challenge in this book. The division between "real" and "virtual" nonetheless continues to bear the appearance of common sense. A "real" relationship is one marked by countless day-to-day encounters. It is defined by shared experiences and memories. One's relationship with a childhood friend is "real." Relationships with siblings and parents are "real" and recognisable, even if they have been interrupted by years of absence. Even relationships with colleagues or neighbours can be understood as real and grievable. Virtual relationships, however, have not yet become so common or accepted as to be broadly recognised as real in the same sense.

Virtual family relationships add another level of complexity insofar as they are open to claims of fictionalisation. Even within SL we encountered people who rejected the reality and value of blended and chosen families for reasons including the fact that they are constructed and occur primarily in virtual spaces. One resident, commenting on what he perceived as the falseness of many SL relationships, asked: "those folks who can't have children in RL, how can they experience that in RL?"

Another resident said that

> I think it's self-deluding crap, a fantasy structured to help them cope. But it's not real. I'm talking for myself, I can't speak for them. But most of those families fall apart. They're a construct out of a need to belong without any real world ties to bind them. Things are ephemeral here.

While SL offers the possibility of a broad range of family compositions, then, they do not go uncontested. Residents we have spoken to have demonstrated a variety of perspectives on the reality of relationships formed in SL. Few residents suggested that romantic relationships are inherently and inescapably unreal. Family relationships, however, are more open to

[12] Hensley, 127.

[13] "For Whom the Ontology Turns: Theorizing the Digital Real," *Current Anthropology* 57, no. 4 (August 2016): 387–407, https://doi.org/10.1086/687362.

question. This suggests a sensitivity to the boundaries of kinship which is potentially a response to changing cultures of relatedness outside of SL. Kinship is a social construct as well as biological interpretation in which ideas of relatedness and responsibility are understood and enacted.[14] The rise of new reproductive technologies, feminism, and queer politics has been central to the denaturalisation of kinship locus in the nuclear family in Western cultures.[15] The experiences of respondents who do feel a high level of relatedness with SL family members even where no legal or biological ties exist thus speak not to a unique phenomenon but to changing ideas about what a family is within Western contexts.

These experiences also speak to the development of what we term digital flesh—the layering of experiences over time which serve to transform the avatar into a fully fleshed moral actor, able to form significant and meaningful attachments and subject to moral harm. Not all residents develop this digital flesh. Those whose engagement with SL is limited either in terms of time spent in-world or willingness to connect with other residents are less likely to reach this point of complete moral engagement and presence in SL. The digital flesh is, in a sense, the sum of the attachments and experiences of connection a resident-as-avatar encounters in SL. Digital flesh is, for some residents, solidified through the processes of family formation and the experiences associated with interconnectedness in family groupings.

Romantic Partnerships

One of the key forms of familial relationships in SL is romantic partnerships, including spousal relationships. This is a type of relationship which has been prevalent and commented upon since the very first social virtual worlds. Turkle illustrated the romantic potential of virtual worlds in 1994

[14] Janet Carsten, ed., "Introduction – Cultures of Relatedness," in *Cultures of Relatedness: New Approaches to the Study of Kinship* (Cambridge [England] New York: Cambridge University Press, 2000), 3.

[15] Carsten, 13; Sarah Franklin and Helena Ragone, *Reproducing Reproduction: Kinship, Power, and Technological Innovation* (University of Pennsylvania Press, 1998); Sarah Franklin and Susan McKinnon, *Relative Values: Reconfiguring Kinship Studies* (Duke University Press, 2002); Sarah Franklin, "Biologization Revisited: Kinship Theory in the Context of the New Biologies," in *Relative Values*, by Janet Carsten and Gillian Feeley-Harnik, ed. Sarah Franklin and Susan McKinnon (Duke University Press, 2002), 302–25, https://doi.org/10.1215/9780822383222-012.

with the story of Peter, a 23-year-old graduate student in physics whose only romantic relationships had occurred in MUDs, or Multi-User Dungeons, early, generally text-based, roleplaying games.[16] Relationships in SL must be understood in terms of this lengthy history as well as in relation to existing media discourses linking virtual lifestyles to sexuality and at times to sexual deviancy. In SL romance is an accepted aspect of social life. For some residents these romantic partnerships can be transferred offline. Samantha and Louis met in a Korean themed sim in 2006. Samantha recalled her feelings during the early stage of their relationship:

> The excitement of meeting someone in this way. Not knowing then what either of us looked like in RL. Or our RL names etc. Or ages. And hearing his voice first as there was no voice then. So I only heard him once he did a DJ gig.

The two quickly began to spend hours each day talking to one another. A year and a half later, they were living together offline. Louis asked an SL friend to design a tattoo of the avatars they had used when they met. This partnership became more real for both Louis and Samantha through its transition to the physical world. Their emotional connection, forged in an environment in which interactions were mediated through avatar bodies, survived the transition to one in which interactions were mediated through physical bodies. Once this transition was complete, they no longer saw themselves as being in an SL relationship. Instead, SL became part of their personal narrative of togetherness.

Some residents suggest that romantic relationships in the virtual world are more authentic than those in the physical world due to the removal of physical markers of difference—including markers of disability but also more mundane differences such as variation in height—which may prevent partnerships from forming in another context.

James, the leader of a virtual yoga ashram, met his wife in SL. He told the story of meeting a woman in the ashram, forming a bond, and eventually meeting in "real life" and getting married. He believed that this was a relationship which could not have emerged outside of SL: partly because his wife lived in Holland, while he was in the USA but also because of

[16] Sherry Turkle, "Constructions and Reconstructions of Self in Virtual Reality: Playing in the MUDs," *Mind, Culture, and Activity* 1, no. 3 (June 1994): 161–62, https://doi.org/10.1080/10749039409524667.

social norms relating to physical stature and compatibility. He stated that "[s]he is tall, 5′9" and I'm short 5′3" so we would never have gotten together in RL probably." Meeting in SL embodied as avatars, the two were able to connect on a spiritual and an emotional level without the intrusion of these norms associated with the physical world. The power of the avatar as a means of representing the self, outside of the limitations of actual physical embodiment, is such that it allows for a different form of first impression based on chosen representation rather than factors such as genetics or class. For James and his wife, the connection formed in this environment was lasting. At the time of our meeting, the pair had been married for a month, and James was in the process of moving to Holland. This was the culmination of a five-and-a-half-year relationship. The romance which James believed would not have emerged had the physical body been the mediator in their initial interaction survived the substitution of the imperfect physical embodiment for the carefully constructed avatars. That this served to strengthen their attachment speaks to the continued power and significance of corporeality. It also demonstrates the potential of SL to disrupt ideas of compatibility and attraction associated with bodily norms. The presence of an existing intellectual and emotional relationship smoothed out some of the awkwardness which may otherwise have been associated with their first meeting.

These narratives demonstrate that, for many residents, the ultimate goal of relationships formed in SL is to be transferred to offline. This act of transference alters romantic relationships, rendering them more real in a sense than those carried out solely through SL. The desire for such a transition speaks to the power of the ontological categories of firstness and secondness as they relate to romantic relationships. These continue to define "real" romance in a way that is not necessarily relevant to friendships or other family relationships. The importance of the romantic partner as the "first" or most significant relationship in a person's life renders this relationship one that is uniquely linked to the firstness of the physical world. Not every SL romance leads to the development of a relationship outside of SL and, indeed, the experiences of our research participants suggest Samantha, Louis, and James are in a minority. Many residents told us stories of heartbreak and deception. Shane, who states that he rarely uses SL but maintains an account to pay for the land used by a mental health support group, described the pain caused by untruth in virtual relationships. The following interview abstract, edited for clarity, demonstrates the very real pain that Shane has experienced. It also provides a rare example of a resident who believes that SL relationships are almost necessarily unreal.

> Shane: I've mourned the death of truth as people take on personas and prey on others. Letting ourselves get too attached to an idea of a person. Self-deluding pap. One of the other things with SL 'relationships' is that they are entered into rather quickly for the sake of feeling part of something, feeling loved. It's the idea of it rather than something stable, real and healthy.
>
> Clara Coates (kittyrissa): I wonder if that's why they involve so much drama?
>
> Shane: Of course. Think of any RL relationship that is rushed into. Anything rushed into is just as easily rushed out of. In Second Life there are other factors that play into it, drama can be amplified. People think they'll find something here they're missing out there [in 'real life']. They think that they can play around without it really being 'cheating.' They think it's not 'real' so it doesn't 'count.' I have a friend who has been with her boyfriend for five years. She met him here. So it's not completely outside the realm of possibility. But they're not the norm. I have been in an SL relationship and allowed myself those blinders. It sucked finding out it was a lie.
>
> Clara Coates (kittyrissa): Would you be willing to tell me about it?
>
> Shane: Yeah, I suppose so. It was a few years ago? Longer. Time stretches. There was kind of a slow build over a couple months I think. She was always very guarded. Maybe I liked trying to break that down? I'm not sure. Pretty much everything she fed me was bullshit.
>
> Clara Coates (kittyrissa): What sort of bullshit?
>
> Shane: Anything about her, what she'd been through, who she was, photographs. We talked on Skype and such. Then one of my associates on SL messages me out of the blue and wakes me up by saying "she's lying etc." I look into it and sure enough it's true. I confront her and she cuts me off because the illusion has been shattered. For her there was no point in addressing it because it didn't matter. The masquerade was over.
>
> Clara Coates (kittyrissa): That must have been painful.
>
> Shane: Quite. I felt pretty stupid.
>
> Clara Coates (kittyrissa): How did you deal with it?
>
> Shane: A lot of moping and feeling sorry for myself. A lot of grief and anger. I skipped denial. A whole lot of anger

Shane stated that this experience made him feel stupid. He stated that he was a "rational adult" who let himself "believe in the fantasy." The fantasy in this case was a constructed life which he was led to believe existed outside of SL. Even when speaking to us years later, he could not work out why his former partner had deceived him. Shane saw the first life identity of this former partner as central to their relationship. To lie about that identity was to be dishonest in the most important way. He interpreted his partner's behaviour after she was revealed to be untruthful about her offline identity as a sign that she did not care about him or about her own deception. Whether this is an accurate analysis is impossible to determine. Shane said that many of his friends had similar experiences. One of these friends was a transwoman who had been in a long-term relationship with a person who claimed to have been diagnosed with cancer. The person making this claim was believed to have died. That person was discovered to be a fiction constructed by a couple sharing an avatar. From Shane's perspective, SL relationships were dangerous and potentially damaging. Claims to truth or authenticity in such relationships were inherently suspect due to the prevalence of residents who were untruthful about their first life identities. Emotional investment in such a relationship was a likely predictor of heartache and grief.

Ken, a resident who runs a successful SL real estate development company, told his own story of deception and heartache. He was involved in a three-year SL marriage to someone he described as "the perfect woman." The pair was, he believed, very much in love. They spoke about marrying in the physical world. He stated that

> One day she wasn't there anymore. A year later, I was able to contact her, and come to find out that she thought simply disappearing would somehow make it easier to me to move on. I had to clarify to her that it was the opposite, and that she should never do that to someone. At the time, she was fighting cancer, and had to care for her family. I had to give her space. But her space turned into a year of no communication. I couldn't communicate with her outside of SL so I didn't know if she had succumbed to the cancer, or was lying in a ditch somewhere. We were close, we had spoken by phone, but she also stopped answering her phone. In the letters I wrote her, I told her all I could do was accept her decision. And not communicating was a decision. And I wished her the best.

Ken also said that SL relationships could never act as a long-term alternative to relationships in the real world. He said that "reality will always be your first life." This is reflected in his desire to meet his SL wife offline and to marry her in "real life." Ken implied in his narrative that he had forgotten the significance of reality when he made the decision to pursue a romantic relationship in SL. However, his own story, and his stated objective in terms of this significant relationship, suggests that he had always put "reality" before SL in relation to a hierarchy of meaningful emplacement in which a relationship could be carried out.

These stories reveal a sense among residents that the true self is the self known and knowable outside of SL. Some level of deception—such as failing to reveal one's true height—may be acceptable so long as it does not speak to the heart of who one *is*. They also reveal a belief among many residents that the purpose or value of a romantic relationship formed in SL lies in its capacity to be transformed into a relationship offline. This speaks to prevalent ideas about the nature of romantic relationships in SL but also elsewhere—a kind of shared imaginary which is exaggerated in this virtual context. This imaginary privileges not only firstness as the touchstone of a meaningful romantic relationship but also monogamy as the only truly fulfilling type of romantic connection. However, residents who are deeply embedded in SL—who have developed digital flesh—may form a different type of relationship. The following story suggests that SL relationships should be approached with more nuance—that it is possible for a relationship carried out entirely in SL to be fulfilling and, moreover, to exist alongside and in full knowledge of pre-existing physical relationships. Laura, who runs and curates an art gallery, told us about her online relationship with a SL artist, Elliot. The pair had met at an art exhibition and quickly fallen in love. They decided to create their own gallery space in which they could showcase Elliott's sculptures and the works of other artists they admired. Laura and Elliot pair were members of a broad artistic community including curators, gallery owners, photographers, and other artists.

Laura and Elliot enjoyed a relationship which spanned five years. During this time, they worked together as business partners and lived as lovers. Laura said that, for SL relationships to last, the couple must have a mutual goal and shared interests. This is suggestive of quite a utilitarian approach to relationships. It is, however, reflective of the nature of long-term romantic relationships offline in which couples tend to share goals and interests, financial or otherwise. For Laura and Elliot, the interest was art. Elliot was a talented sculptor, creating beautiful work using an array of building techniques. He built and designed the gallery space. Laura organised events and ran PR campaigns. Their art never made them money. It was a shared passion which bound them together.

At the time Laura met Elliot, she had already experienced heartbreak in SL relationships. She stated that

> It is so long ago. It happens to so many people here in Second Life. You meet a person here. You talk, you get intimate, you share a lot and it hurts when that is ended by the other person. I had an Italian BF [boyfriend] long ago. He stopped our relationship because he felt he was cheating on his RL wife. He was in love. He didn't want to see me. Hurt him too much.

Laura did not view SL relationships as the equivalent to those formed offline and in this important sense she differed from her former partner. For her, having an SL relationship did not imply cheating as such on a RL spouse. This speaks to a different orientation to morality and reality in relation to SL sexuality than that held by many other residents. This negative relationship experience, along with others, had led her to a state which she described as "SL mature"—this meant that she had experienced some of the difficulties and dramas involved in SL relationships and that she was prepared for something more solid. Laura's "SL mature" state, while she meant it to refer to her experience of romantic relationships specifically, speaks to our concept of the "digital flesh" insofar as she saw herself as having become a moral and responsible individual-as-avatar as a direct result of her online experiences. Both Laura and Elliot had partners in the physical world. Both of their partners were aware of their SL relationship—though not, Laura states, of its sexual nature. She did not speculate on how her partner might respond if he was aware of this aspect of her relationship with Elliot. The two couples met in Paris under difficult circumstances.

Laura was devastated to learn, four years into the relationship, that Elliot had been diagnosed with cancer. He was not yet 50. Four months later she and her real-life partner travelled from their home in the UK to Elliot's home in Paris, where they spent time with his family. She described the experience as "strange," saying:

> It was nice and sort of strange to meet him in RL. You know a lot about each other and then you see each other face to face. Strange. Afterwards it was strange to meet in SL again and kiss and make love because in the back of our minds we knew that we met in RL with our partners.

Laura found that her partner was comfortable with her SL relationship. Both of her relationships—with her offline partner and with Elliot—seemed permanent. They were compatible with one another. This was true to the extent that her RL partner—the man with whom she shared her "first life"—was willing to travel with her to meet the person with whom she was partnered in her "second" life. Whether this would have been the case if her RL partner was aware of the sexual nature of her SL relationship remains an unanswered question. However, the fact that Laura and Elliott saw meeting physically as necessary suggests that both retained a sense that authentic connections required or were enhanced by some sort of physical association. Their sexual and romantic relationship could survive as an important part of their lives through the meeting of their digital flesh, but their close friendship, particularly in the face of death, needed to be solidified through the touchstone of the real.

A year after Elliot's cancer diagnosis, just months after Laura met him for the first time, Elliot died. Laura described the final months of their relationship:

> He got the message in December 2014 and died in November 2015. All that time, except for the last months when he was so ill he couldn't sit long and later couldn't come to SL at all, we talked. I stood by him.
>
> […]
>
> The last time Elliot was in SL he was in his sick bed. His son had placed his laptop close to him. It was the opening of the exhibit where some of his posters were exhibited next to the amazing photographs of [some Second Life photographers].

She said of his death:

> I miss him but I had time to get used to the fact that he would be gone. One year. His cancer ate him slowly. Same as in RL. When a dear one dies suddenly by an accident for instance it is so much more difficult to get over than when you have the time to say goodbye. And Elliot and I had that time.

Laura describes herself as a "SL widow." She doesn't want another online relationship. She continues to run the gallery she and Elliot designed together. She displays his artworks and shows them to interested visitors. She spends time with their mutual friends. For Laura, this SL partnership was important and enduring. It was a love—one which was able to cross national borders and to coexist alongside another, physical, relationship.

Sarah also lost an online partner. She had been in an emotionally intense and turbulent relationship for some years with Michael, a man she had met only in SL. When Sarah asked to meet Michael offline, he declined, telling her that their relationship would never be transferred offline. This made her suspicious about his true identity, but, despite this, their relationship continued. Sarah and Michael were forming a romantic attachment in the midst of a popular preoccupation with the unreality of such attachments. This concern has been the subject of a popular documentary and MTV series, both entitled *Catfish*. The very term "catfishing" has entered the lexicon as a descriptor of an activity wherein a person presents a false identity to someone they have met online, usually in the context of a romantic partnership. In this context, Sarah found Michael's reticence about meeting offline to be a very distressing aspect of their relationship. It spoke not only of the potential unreality of his persona but also of an unwillingness or inability to provide what Sarah felt she needed from him—a "real" relationship. The enduring nature of this romantic attachment in the face of a seemingly insurmountable incompatibility—this disagreement on the world in which the relationship would be played out—demonstrates the depth of the affection Sarah felt for Michael and her willingness to overlook her own needs in favour of meeting his. It also provides evidence of the impossibility of meeting the needs of both parties to a relationship where one party views the offline real as the ultimate destination for a true and meaningful partnership and the other sees SL as a valid or preferable space of connection. Michael's refusal to valorise the real, or firstness over secondness, meant that Sarah was forced to choose between her own moral prioritisation of the real and her desire to be with Michael. She chose to try to be satisfied with the connection based in digital flesh.

Michael's pattern of SL use was consistent. The virtual world was an important space in which he was able to escape, to form meaningful friendships, and to play out his dreams of becoming a musician. His digital flesh was well established, and in a sense his loved ones believe that his second life was more fulfilling than his first. Michael had schizophrenia. Mental health problems were something he and Sarah had discussed at length. Sarah, who lives with PTSD and severe anxiety, found in Michael someone who was able to understand her struggles and in whom she was able to confide. Michael was open and honest with her about his problems and the impact they had on his life. He lived on a disability pension and, while he did enjoy social connections with friends and family offline, nonetheless felt isolated. When he suddenly stopped appearing online, Sarah and her friends were concerned. His established pattern of use and their knowledge of his mental health concerns led them to believe that something significant had occurred. None of Michael's SL friends knew him offline, leaving a community of loved ones frightened and confused.

Sarah did not know Michael's "real," or offline, name. They exclusively used their screen names when talking to and about one another. They had spoken about the details of their offline lives only rarely. Theirs had been a relationship in which nothing was closed except for that information which would enable them to identify and find one another offline. Sarah knew Michael's most intimate secrets and fears, yet she did not know his name. The most specific detail available to her was the name of the town in which he lived. Sarah realised that in order to gain closure she would need to investigate Michael's fate. Her act of searching went further than emails or Google searches—Sarah combed the announcements of funeral homes in and around her partner's home town until she found a notice announcing the funeral of a man who was the right age, and had passed away at the right time, to be Michael. From the information in this notice, she was able to track down his Facebook page and speak to members of his family. A relative was able to confirm Michael's identity and to tell Sarah that he had died peacefully in his sleep. This experience was bittersweet. Sarah was able to gain closure, to share the news with her online community, and to mourn. Equally importantly, she was able to certify that Michael was, in the offline world, the person he had claimed to be. This had been a major concern for most of their relationship and had led to fights between them. To discover that Michael had not deceived her—that he was really the man he had claimed to be and that his life was as he had described it—retrospectively rendered their partnership more meaningful. Sarah had not been catfished. Further, she found that his family was aware of his friends and loved ones in SL. This provided her with a sense that Michael's online relationships, with herself and with his many friends, were indeed important to him. The vast quantity of time he spent online in life was not sufficient to demonstrate this to Sarah. It was only by discovering that his "real" family were aware of his virtual life that Sarah was able to develop a sense of her own significance to Michael. Despite the fact that their relationship was never transferred to the "real" world, Sarah still judged its validity by measuring the extent to which it formed part of the narrative Michael's offline loved ones told about his life. The touchstone of the first or physical world did not lose its power for Sarah. However, its meaning altered. She could never have a physical partnership with Michael, but she could feel assured that the digital partnership they had enjoyed formed a place in his primary narrative of self.

Becoming Family

In our research the most common form of constructed family relationship was sibling relationships. The stories of two sibling dyads, told by the surviving sibling after the death of the other, help to explain the way in which these relationships form and the enduring impact they can have. The first of these pairs, Mystique and Lila, met on a roleplay sim based on the *Anita Blake: Vampire Hunter* books by author Laurell K. Hamilton. Mystique described the books as erotic vampire fiction and stated that it was the sexual aspect of vampirism which first drew her to the community. This is in a sense in keeping with the salacious media depictions of SL. However, this eroticism was not sufficient to hold her attention over a long period of time. Over time Mystique began to lose interest in this aspect of the roleplay and became more concerned with the culture and aesthetic of vampirism. In a sense the sexual play which brought her to SL and to the vampire roleplay community more specifically lost its novelty, and she remained due to the other emotional and relational investments she had made. Her avatar is pale, with platinum blonde hair and fangs. Lila was also a SL vampire. She was an established member of the community when Mystique joined SL. "She was one of the first friends I met on here," Mystique said. "We just got along immediately." There was no clear moment at which the relationship between the two ceased to be a close friendship and became something more intimate. "We just started calling each other sister." There was a sense that this was natural and that the closeness of their relationship necessitated or at least itself justified the nomenclature of relatedness. This is demonstrative of the fluidity that characterises relationships in SL. In a world that prioritises digital connections rather than those rooted in biology, the terminology associated with relatedness can be more easily applied to persons who may elsewhere be classed as close friends.

Edmund met Sam in 2012, at which point Sam had been in SL for a year and Edmund several months. Like Mystique and Lila, the pair got along immediately. Sam was online most of the time and soon revealed to Edmund that he was in a rehab facility after losing a leg. He was unable to participate in many activities in RL, and SL was his way of being in the world rather than sitting passively in his hospital bed. SL offered both escape and connection. Sam introduced Edmund to Gorean roleplay. The Gorean community revolves around a mythology based on a series of science fiction novels by John Norman. An important aspect of this community is master/slave roleplay, and this was something both Sam and Edmund engaged in. Their relationship, however, was always platonic. It was an intense, but not sexual, friendship. "Once we'd met, there was no keeping us apart, and in a way that felt like I'd known him for so many years," Edmund told us. After a period of friendship, Sam asked Edmund to be his brother. "It was one of the greatest honours I could imagine," Edmund said. He had no difficulty accepting the sibling relationship, saying "it just made sense that we must have grown up together." The idea that the relationship "made sense" is suggestive of the intuitive nature of SL family construction. Families do not come to be because of any careful planning or deliberation. They are instead usually formed organically, particularly where the relationship in question is a sibling relationship. These familial ties are formed because they "feel right" or "make sense." The idea of feeling as though SL siblings have "grown up together" is not one we have encountered in the narratives of other interviewees. However, this assertion should not be read as false or an affectation. Edmund was tapping into a popular imaginary positioning siblings as uniquely similar as a result of their shared upbringing. His belief that it made sense to imagine that he and Sam had grown up together suggests a sympathy of thought and feeling which was understood by both Edmund and Sam as a natural indicator of relatedness.

The residents involved in constructing these families did so as mature adults. Edmund was 37 years of age at the time of our interview. Sam died at the age of 49. Mystique was 41 when interviewed, and Lila died at 52. Their imagined shared childhoods were projected far back into their personal histories. They were also relationships situated in a context in which all of the residents were engaged in roleplay. Sam and Edmund formed a close bond in the context of the Gorean community, while Mystique and Lila both roleplayed as vampires. They shared aspects of their offline lives with their sibling pairs, but they primarily interacted as selves which were in important ways "true" selves but which nonetheless were intentionally created and constructed selves. Both Edmund and Mystique describe their sibling relationship as being characterised by emotional intimacy. While Edmund was able to meet Sam in RL twice, Mystique's relationship with Lila existed entirely in SL. This distinction does not appear to be matched by a distinction in the significance of the two relationships. Both Edmund and Mystique regularly communicated with their deceased siblings, and both described their deaths as a significant loss. Notably, both interviewees had constructed places in which they were able to feel a continuing connection to their siblings. The bond they felt with their SL siblings did not exist merely in the "here and now" of the moments in which the relationship was enacted. These sibling relationships, constructed through and mediated by the screen, came to form important parts of their narratives of self.

Some SL families include members who are not people at all in the sense of a person existing "behind the screen." For Ellie, SL is a place where she can live peacefully. "My life [in SL is] very pretty lol. And it is not complicated. RL is complicated. SL is an escape." Her avatar has tanned skin, flowing blonde hair, and exaggerated curves. She designed it to look like Barbie, and she sees her home as something akin to a reproduction of Barbie's Dream House. Ellie is the married mother of teenagers in RL but has chosen, in SL, to form a virtual marriage and family. Her RL marriage is not monogamous and her husband sat beside her when she married her SL husband, David. David, a married father of adult children in RL, has to sneak online when his RL wife is not watching. His relationship is more traditional and has already been jeopardised by his online romances. Whether David views his marriage to Ellie as a form of infidelity is unclear—it is, however, evident that his wife sees it in this way. The categories of firstness and secondness do not preclude the relationship existing in the virtual space as being seen as a threat to that which exists in the physical world. David's decision to transgress the boundaries of his RL relationship in order to form a SL family potentially speaks to the discourses of infidelity and falsehood that have been traditionally associated with media depictions of SL. However, the very normality of the family life Ellie and David have constructed serves to contradict those discourses.

When Ellie and David decided to start a SL family, adopting a child from one of the many agencies pairing residents roleplaying children with potential parents was not an option. Ellie said:

> I don't judge people who portray children, but I am not comfortable near them. I want my adult Barbie world to be for adults lol. I've known a few child avatars and in all cases but one, I think there were some very strong mental concerns.

Ellie's characterisation of SL as an "adult Barbie world" does not indicate that she views SL as insignificant or unimportant. In fact, Ellie spends a great deal of time, money, and energy in SL, both in her personal life and in her role as an educator. The fact that Ellie wants this world to be exclusively for adults seems to indicate an orientation towards SL as a rare and valuable space in which adults can play freely. That is, she welcomes this as a space in which play itself can be a serious and adult practice outside of medicalised and pathologised discourses relating to adult play. While Ellie wished to play at family life in SL, she saw bringing actual children into such an environment as antithetical to the promotion of a space in which adult play could retain its legitimacy. To play as a child, for her, involves crossing the boundaries of propriety and opening oneself, and by extension the virtual world, up to investigation and diagnosis by a medicalising gaze. The solution to the tension between Ellie's desire for SL children and her discomfort around adults who portray children was to form a family using prim babies—animated babies which are able to interact with avatars and the environment. These can be acquired at adoption agencies and purchased in a store, or, if a resident wishes, they can attach a "pregnancy HUD[17]" and see their avatars become pregnant and give birth. A wide range of prim babies are available, and these boast varying levels of sophistication. Generally, however, they can be fed, changed, and comforted, and they have needs which must be met. Some prim babies can only perform certain interactions with the avatar assigned as their owner. This can lead to an enforced division of labour in which only one SL parent is able to perform some of the tasks required to care for the child.

Ellie and David have three prim babies. One was born through the use of a pregnancy HUD. One was adopted from another resident, "a girl who had to leave SL because her RL husband gave her a choice," and one was adopted from an agency. The idea that virtual children can be adopted and indeed ought to be adopted where their parent is no longer to be present in SL speaks to the moral value that these items can acquire. They are not merely objects but digital children, requiring parental care. Ellie's babies are all Zooby brand, and all are owned by Ellie. David's avatar is able to feed and change all three babies, but he cannot pick them up and is therefore unable to meet their need for affection. In order to overcome

[17] Heads Up Display, an item which attaches to the avatar. These have different functions. In this case, the HUD allows the resident to control the pregnancy and provides them with messages relating to the pregnancy and foetus.

this, David sometimes logs on to Ellie's SL account. He does a lot of the care work required for these virtual children, then, but must do so—due to the constraints set by their designer—as their mother. The in-world primary caregiver is Ellie—a female avatar—but she is at times operated or inhabited by someone other than the primary typist who uses Ellie. There is a crossing over of type of roleplay which has become a defining feature of the familial relationship Ellie and David share with their digital children.

These very different means of forming families in SL draw into question what it means to be a family and how family ought to be understood and valued. It is clear that "family" means different things to different SL residents. These families contain layers of friendship, of strong emotional ties, and in fact of roleplay. They are just a few of the many family configurations that have been adopted by residents.

We wish to touch only briefly upon the subject of taboo families. This is not an area we have researched in any depth, yet the shadow of such family formations problematises the parent-child relationships in other constructed and blended families. Just as we have encountered adoption agencies in-world, we have found taboo adoption agencies—spaces in which people who wish to roleplay as parents or children in sexual relationships are able to find one another. This gives credence to the assertions of residents such as Ellie who assert that paedophilia, or paedophilic roleplay, occurs within SL. It also creates problems for residents who wish to engage in family roleplay involving non-sexual relationships with family members who are child avatars operated by adult typists. Where some parent-child roleplay relationships and adoption agencies promote or accept forms of paedophilia, all such relationships and agencies become open to suspicion.

Doing and Displaying Family

The academic concept of "doing family" is adopted from the feminist notion of "doing gender."[18] The idea that family is something that must be done suggests that families are inherently fragile rather than necessarily strong and connected and that they must be constructed and reconstructed

[18] Margaret K. Nelson, "Single Mothers 'Do' Family," *Journal of Marriage and Family* 68, no. 4 (November 2006): 782, https://doi.org/10.1111/j.1741-3737.2006.00292.x.

through intentional interactional work.[19] Nelson notes that, for single mothers, "doing family" requires not just giving but also denying, having the power to say "no."[20] This right, which is so significant, can be ceded to a partner in order to support the construction of a nuclear family.[21] This potentially speaks to the continuing power of traditional modes of family life in the ways in which family is "done." It also speaks to the power to give and to withhold as a key attribute of family. This is an attribute that is impossible to retain or, at the very least, problematised in a situation in which a family consists of adult engaged in roleplay. The power to give or deny in such circumstances can only ever be illusory, a tool used in play.

Finch argues that families must be not just done but also displayed. By this she means that there is a fundamentally social aspect to family life wherein actions only constitute family practices if they are understood by relevant others as doing so.[22] This is made more important in a contemporary context wherein family cannot be understood in clearly defined boundaries, such as the home one inhabits.[23] The same action may be read either as display or not a display depending on the context. If an activity is embedded in the routines of family life, it is an act of doing family but not a display. The same activity, where relationships or routine is less established, may be display.[24] In SL families are almost invariably constructed and seen to be constructed. This leaves them open to contestation and requires that family is done and displayed in innovative ways.

Sophie, the mother of a large SL blended family, demonstrates aspects of both doing and displaying family ties in her routine practice. She emphasised the enduring and genuine emotional ties between herself and her family members.

> Each person in the family is unique. I met some recently, some years and years ago. Some I even brought here with me from another game. They are like real family to me. I love them dearly.

[19] Suzanne Bianchi, "Mothers and Daughters 'Do,' Fathers 'Don't Do' Family: Gender and Generational Bonds," *Journal of Marriage and Family* 68, no. 4 (2006): 812.

[20] Nelson, "Single Mothers 'Do' Family," 793.

[21] Nelson, 794.

[22] "Displaying Families," *Sociology* 41, no. 1 (February 2007): 66, https://doi.org/10.1177/0038038507072284.

[23] Finch, 68.

[24] Finch, 79.

Family relationships are reiterated and reconstructed through daily group activity. Sophie and her family run a virtual farm. These farms can be incredibly sophisticated, featuring animals which not only move but respond to actions, which can mate, and which can be slaughtered for food. They can also feature crops which must be tended and facilities for cooking, building, and crafting. While SL avatars are not designed with physical needs—they cannot, in their ordinary state, become hungry or sick—some communities have created HUDs which modify their avatars to require food or other objects. Virtual farms produce the food for these communities. Frequent interaction with the many plants and animals on SL farms is required in order to ensure production. Sophie stated that this is a family endeavour which requires the participation of all members. She said "we all chip in to help on chores and such. The kids earn allowances. It's really cute. And we use the farm to supply one of the family stores we have." The act of doing and displaying family through the work of running a farm and a family store suggests that family life is associated for Sophie and her kin associate familiness with a type of rural imaginary wherein children are active and necessary contributors to the family economy. More quintessentially modern forms of family wherein children attend school and parents work, with members of families enjoying relatively separate but interrelated lives, do not seem to be desirable in this roleplay context. The family form practiced here is idealised and sentimentalised.

Sophie emphasised the ordinariness of virtual family life. When not working on the farm, she and her children watch movies together, play games, or go shopping. They do, she said, "anything a normal family would do." In this we can see evidence both of "doing" family through engaging in regular routine interactions and of "displaying" family through her emphasis on such interactions as part of family relations. The rural and urban ideals of family life combine to contribute to the construction of an idealised imaginary. There are, however, aspects of life within Sophie's constructed family, however, which are without parallel in the physical world. Some of Sophie's children have multiple SL accounts. In some cases, she is the mother of the same person on multiple accounts. This means that there are two or more avatars which are recognised as the children of Sophie's avatar but which are in fact operated by one person. This, she said, makes it difficult to report precisely how many children she has.

The second unparalleled aspect of SL family life is the fact that Sophie's children are roleplaying. She is constantly aware that her children are in fact adults who choose to engage with the virtual world in child bodies. There is therefore a need to construct a relationship on two levels—foremost, the relationship is that of mother and child—but in addition there is another relationship formed between the adults who are behind the avatars. This raises questions of identity and of "acting one's age." The following interview segment highlights the way Sophie and her family deal with these issues.

> Clara Coates (kittyrissa): So you said that you have SL children—how do you interact with them? Do they act their child age most of the time?
> Sophie: it depends on if they are in character or not
> Sophie: and depends on their rp [roleplay] age and rl age
> Sophie: the small young children will act their age when in character
> Sophie: but there are times they are ooc [out of character]
> Sophie: when they act like their rl selves
> Sophie: it's not just role play for us
> Sophie: we're all close friends out of game too
> Sophie: so I know both sides of them
> Sophie: the older kids just act themselves all the time

By asserting that the members of her family are "all close friends" outside of SL, Sophie provides evidence of the reality of her family relationships. She suggests that an intimacy exists both when family members are "in character" and when they are "out of character." These layers of "in character" and "out of character" are complicated further by the fact that Sophie's SL siblings, unlike her children, are people whom she knows in RL. One is her RL sister, the others she describes as "like best friends." Thus all of Sophie's family members are people she knows in multiple capacities—as children who are also adults or as embodied loved ones in a physical world who bear a different, if similar, relationship to Sophie when encountered in SL.

Despite or perhaps because of the complicated and multilayered nature of this blended family grouping, Sophie displays family by reiterating the work she does to maintain her relationships. "It's very much like a real family," she said, "we have ups and downs. People have arguments and make up. We love and cry together." She demonstrated an awareness of the importance of "doing" family, stating:

> Just like in RL it takes effort to create bonds with people. Just 'cause you're born into a family doesn't mean that you're going to be close to those people. You have to take the time and interest to build that bond. SL families are the same way. They don't just start out all peaches and cream. You have to work at them. Nothing good comes easy. But in the end its definitely worth the effort.

For Sophie, then, the "reality" of her blended family is legitimated in part by the work she and others do in maintaining loving relationships. This work, which mirrors forms of doing and displaying family offline, is seen as more important in performing this legitimating function than traditional biological or legal markers through which kinship is often defined.

Losing Family

Mystique's SL sister Lila committed suicide in RL. Lila had been struggling with problems for some time. She had recently lost a job. The final straw, Mystique said, was when Lila's heart was broken by her SL partner. The pair agreed to meet at his home in Massachusetts. It was only when she arrived that she discovered she had been given a fake address. Her partner had lied to her about both his career—he was not in the Navy—and where he lived—he was in fact in Washington. Mystique said:

> She drove all the way to meet him and he wasn't even in the state. A few days after she returned home she drank too much and took a lot of pills.

Mystique did not reflect much on the cruelty inherent in this action. Lila had attempted to combine her SL romance with her offline life, and the result had been heartbreak. Tricking a person who had lost their job into driving interstate—an expensive endeavour—only to leave them alone and disappointed is an act of such cruelty that, had it occurred without the mediating factor of the internet, could not have gone without comment. Mystique appeared to accept this cruelty as something which could be expected where a romantic relationship was formed in SL. This is suggestive of the dominance of the fear of "catfishing" where individuals form SL relationships. "Catfishing" is understood as unfortunate, even cruel, but not outrageous or unexpected. Mystique did, however, believe that this action had contributed to Lila's suicide.

A mutual friend of Mystique and Lila who owned a sim held a memorial service a month after Lila died. Thirty people attended and ten spoke. "It was sad, it was funny," Mystique said. "At her memorial, many people spoke about the fun times that were had." After the memorial service, Mystique created a crypt as a "final resting place" for her sister. This crypt has become her own SL home. "This is where my home is. If I'm not here, I'm in Transylvania or another club. No need for a home anymore." In a sense Mystique lives with Lila. The crypt contains photographs of Lila both in her avatar and physical forms. When Mystique is at her SL home, she is constantly face-to-face with her deceased SL sister. Her ability to construct and live in a space in which she is in such close communication with the dead is associated with her connection to the vampire roleplay community.

Edmund was able to see Sam in RL just before his death. Sam had been ill for some time, the result of complications from a tooth infection which went untreated for too long. There was an early period during which it seemed he would not recover. However, he did. Edmund recalled:

> He woke up, he went back to the rehab facility to get stronger, and as soon as he was there I got a two word text from him: "Please come." I fear hospitals. But I knew that I had to go, and so I got myself together and drove down to Connecticut and prepared myself. I found his room, walked in, and he just took my hand and held it so tightly it almost hurt and we cried together.

Sam recovered completely from this illness. The next spring, he developed kidney problems stemming from diabetes. Edmund did not visit on this occasion, but he was kept informed.

> And he was actually doing better when I got a text from his friend/sister saying that she had something to tell me that I deserved to hear in person rather than over text and I knew then that he was gone. He had been improving, but he threw a blood clot and went from alert and talking to dead in less than fifteen minutes.

Just before hearing the news, Edmund had begun building a chapel for his sim—he and Sam shared a love of building, and it was something he wanted to share with his brother when he was able to come back online. He continued constructing this as a memorial, and it remains on his land, an imposing stone building full of photographs. Edmund visits the chapel when he feels alone and wants to talk to Sam. In this way Sam remains socially alive, part of Edmund's life despite their relationship being in an important sense cut off by the impassable barrier of death. Both Lila and Edmund continued their sibling relationships after being separated by death. These relationships are maintained in SL—in the same world in which they were originally formed. They are, however, maintained in new spaces, places of mourning which were never seen by the siblings who are memorialised.

Care for the Bereaved

The blended and chosen family models created within SL are not necessarily recognisable in other contexts. Where a member of a family formed within SL dies, there is a risk that the grief of those family members who were not connected to the deceased in RL will be disenfranchised. This was not Edmund's experience—his relationship to Sam was recognised by his own RL partner and by Sam's RL friends. However, the narratives of other residents who have lost members of their SL families demonstrate a need to mark this loss through ritual. While this will be discussed in greater detail in later chapters, one example serves to highlight the creative ways in which SL residents care for bereaved partners and family members through ritualising loss.

Sarah's search for her missing partner Michael was detailed earlier in this chapter. After she found out that he had died, she felt overwhelmed—she wanted to do something to mark the loss, but the thought of arranging a memorial service was too confronting. In order to ritualise the loss without putting Sarah under undue pressure, she and some close friends elected to sit shiva for Michael. She was not Jewish and neither was Michael or any member of the group of fellow mourners. This perhaps explains the fact that their version of Shiva did not appear to match that practised in Jewish tradition.[25] Instead, they used the term to denote a mourning process of their own devising in which they sat in an empty building on the virtual replication of New Orleans in which Michael had spent much of his online life. Sarah and a selected group of close friends sat on sofas and reminisced. Michael's virtual dog, which had been outside of his inventory when his avatar logged out of SL for the final time, sat

[25] E.g. "Sitting Shiva," shiva.com, n.d., http://www.shiva.com/learning-center/sitting-shiva/.

with them. Michael had loved this dog and, indeed, had seen it as part of his virtual family. It was the only possession belonging to Michael which remained active in the virtual world, and so its presence during this ritual, and continued presence in the virtual New Orleans, held a special and distinctive meaning. In a sense this ritual was a work of cultural appropriation. In another, it was a creative and immediate response to a grief which demanded recognition. The label "shiva" is in a sense unimportant as anything other than a convenient term used for describing the form the grief of this group took. Its association with religion provided the event with a necessary solemnity.

The blended and chosen families formed within SL are complex, multifaceted, and, above all, meaningful. Whether they are formed between lovers, between close friends who wish to position themselves as siblings, between parents and residents roleplaying as children, or even between a couple and animated objects, these families become part of the daily life of SL residents. They are written into biographies and into understandings of the self. Family construction contributes to the development of the digital flesh which we argue characterises those who have lived full lives in SL. Many SL family relationships will never extend beyond the virtual world. This can render such relationships difficult to explain to those who have no experience of virtual worlds—or, indeed, to less engaged and sympathetic members of SL's own community. Where these complicated family relationships are disrupted or ended by the loss of a member, a situation arises wherein grief must be expressed or marked.

CHAPTER 3

Grievable Lives

Introduction

In James Cameron's 2009 film *Avatar*, a paraplegic former Marine, Jake Sully, is given the opportunity to pilot a physical avatar constructed for his deceased twin brother. The avatar allows him to live and breathe as a Na'vi, a member of a fictional alien race whose planet possesses a mineral desired by humans. As the plot progresses, Sully comes to feel a sense of kinship with the Na'vi and joins with them against the human forces whose mining operation threatens their very lives. Eventually he merges permanently with his avatar, becoming a Na'vi. The film has been criticised for its representations of disability and race and lauded for its anticolonial ethic.[1] For our purposes, it is the representation of the relationship between human and avatar that is most important. Sully is represented as having an unusual ability to connect with and use his avatar. His near immediate mastery of the avatar form has been described as part of the film's promotion of "the myth of the pre-ordained and natural mastery of the attractive young white male."[2] Sully's immediate connection to the avatar and his eventual decision to remain among the Na'vi in his avatar

[1] Si Sheppard, "The Merchant Is Become the Sovereign," *Film International* 13, no. 2 (2015): 41–66.

[2] Robert Hyland, "Going Na'vi: Mastery in Avatar," *Cineaction* 82 (2010): 13.

M. Gibson, C. Carden, *Living and Dying in a Virtual World*,
Palgrave Macmillan Memory Studies,
https://doi.org/10.1007/978-3-319-76099-5_3

embodiment also promote the idea that the avatar can be a means of becoming the true self.

Avatars in this imagining are not deceptive. However, other means of positioning and understanding the avatar form exist. To the extent that one's true self is viewed as an embodied self, the avatar can be understood as a form of disguise. The avatar is therefore a tenuous figure, truthful and deceptive, real and fantasy. These competing narratives and imaginings complicate the position of the avatar in the popular imagination. They render responses to avatar lives and relationships unpredictable.

The avatar lives of SL residents occur in the context of a society which is digitised to the extent that digitisation may be regarded as an unchanging and essential aspect of contemporary social life. Taking up Heidegger's idea that humans are thrown into existence, finding themselves always already "in-and-of the world," Amanda Lagerkvist draws a powerful analogy in the image of our "digital thrownness" in which "our sense of time, memory, space, selfhood, sociality and death are implicated."[3] For Lagerkvist, our digital technologies are existential. They connect us to one another and promise us a form of enduring social presence after death. We are not generally masters of our digitised environments—instead each of us is, as Lagerkvist writes, an "exister," a mortal being embedded in and inextricable from the technologies that make up our lives.[4]

The intimacies and possibilities of self-actualisation afforded by digital technologies make it increasingly difficult to disregard or make fun of emotional connections forged and maintained solely online. However, media sociality without the face-to-face is not an entirely new state of affairs. Before email and text messages there were letters and telegrams. Some of the best-known friendships and partnerships in history were carried out primarily through these media. We may think of Franklin Roosevelt and Winston Churchill, wartime leaders whose extensive correspondence has been described as evidence of a "remarkable friendship."[5] The famous, brilliant, or wealthy have always been permitted the privilege of having lives and connections outside of those associated with the people immediately around them. The rest of us now have no choice but to develop such lives.

[3] Amanda Lagerkvist, "Existential Media: Toward a Theorization of Digital Thrownness," *New Media & Society* 19, no. 1 (January 1, 2017): 97, https://doi.org/10.1177/1461444816649921.

[4] Lagerkvist, 107.

[5] Wolfgang Mieder, "'We Are All in the Same Boat Now' Proverbial Rhetoric in the Churchill-Roosevelt Correspondence," *International Journal of English Studies* 6 (2006): 3.

Judith Butler has highlighted the unequal lenses with which we view human life, asking:

> [W]ho counts as human? Whose lives count as lives? And, finally, what *makes for a grievable life*?[6]

In thinking with these provocations, we argue that what makes life grievable should not diminish or circumscribe the value of lives lived online through avatar embodiments. We make this argument in light of the increasingly digital nature of all our relationships but also in light of the lived experiences, the continuous dwelling, and significant relationships of many of the residents we have met in the course of our research. Avatars in SL develop extensive networks of community members, amass property, and create items that have economic value and emotional both within and outside of the virtual world. They can hold positions of responsibility and trust within their virtual communities. These abilities and commitments, we argue, contribute to the development of digital flesh and the avatar as a moral actor engaged in digital citizenship, community building, and forms of mediatised caregiving.

Living as Avatar

Avatars are common across virtual worlds, including many popular video games. While games such as *Guild Wars 2* and Korean MMO *Black Desert* spruik their advanced character creation options,[7] SL stands apart in the breadth of possibilities open to residents. Avatar bodies do not, like physical bodies, imply the mortality and susceptibility to violence that Butler describes in her essay over the grievability of human lives.[8] Avatar bodies are timeless and ageless, and, in SL, they cannot be physically harmed or killed. Some residents elect to alter their avatars in ways that make them temporarily susceptible to harm. There are areas in SL where it is possible to injure others with weapons, rendering the idea of murder or "avicide"

[6] Judith Butler, "Violence, Mourning, Politics," *Studies in Gender and Sexuality* 4, no. 1 (January 3, 2003): 10, https://doi.org/10.1080/15240650409349213.

[7] "Breaking down Guild Wars 2's Character Creator," Engadget, accessed December 5, 2017, https://www.engadget.com/2012/03/26/breaking-down-guild-wars-2s-character-creator/; "Download the Black Desert Online Character Creator for Free," accessed December 5, 2017, https://www.blackdesertonline.com/events/ccm/.

[8] Butler, "Violence, Mourning, Politics," 15.

part of the broader SL culture just as it is part of the broader gameworld culture of the performativity of death whose counterpart is regeneration. In SL no loss accrues to avatars who are injured, become hungry, or die. They can always be returned to their original state. The vast majority of avatar bodies bear the appearance of youth and athletic good health and thus no visual indication that these bodies are mortal. A resident can live for a decade or longer in a virtual world like SL without their avatar body being marked by time. For MargieG this age-defying embodiment and the aesthetic are visually devoid of the poignancy and mortal countenance of time-bound flesh. However, the avatar is dependent upon the mortal physical body, hidden behind the computer screen.

The relationship between the avatar and the physically embodied person operating it is variable—a participant may have one or many avatars, and a single avatar may be used by one or more people. Theoretically this allows for the possibility that a resident may continue to interact with an avatar after its original operator has died. While we have not heard any stories of this occurring, we must note that it would be difficult for any resident to be aware of such a change unless they were told that it had occurred. Up until this point, we have discussed avatars in a broad and non-specific sense, accepting the self-evident nature of these forms of embodiment. Here we discuss in greater detail what it means to live as an avatar and interact with others through their avatar bodies.

The avatar is an embodiment through which one navigates the social world and relationships with other residents. Avatars play an important role in denoting status—as previous research has demonstrated, certain standard avatar representations indicate that a person is a "newbie," while more complex or curated avatar forms suggest that a person has spent a great deal of time and potentially in-world money on their appearance. Money itself has less meaning in SL than in the physical world in terms of defining the appearance of the embodied self. The vast array of free or almost free body shapes, hairstyles, and items of clothing, alongside the significant capacity for avatar customisation, means that residents who have little financial capital but a working knowledge of the markets of SL may be able to construct their appearance in such a way as to be indistinguishable from those who have invested money in their appearance. Time spent in-world therefore comes to mark avatar appearance and define social status more fully than financial input.

Most residents are familiar with default avatars (see Fig. 3.1 for example) and there is a degree of stigma attached to the use of such avatars,

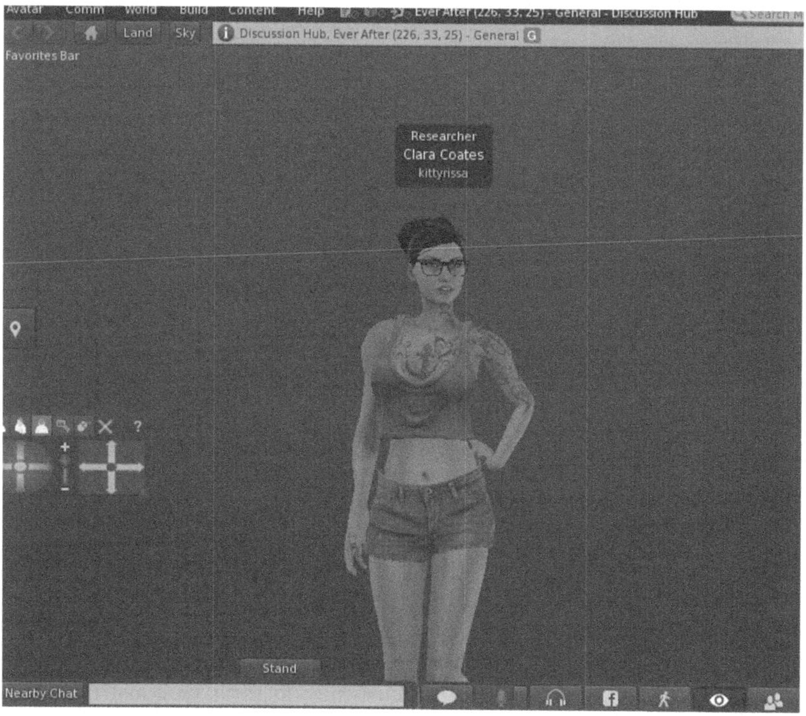

Fig. 3.1 Clara Coates embodied as an unedited default avatar

with residents assuming that anyone with a default appearance is new.[9] While there is a wide variety of potential avatar choices, a desire to portray a true sense of self appears to contribute to the way in which these options are mobilised in the avatar's construction. There is some evidence to suggest that primary avatars—those which a person most often uses—generally look like the "real" person who uses them, with some moderate enhancements which make the avatar more attractive.[10] Some residents have been shown to favour presenting themselves in a way that is entirely authentic,

[9] E.g. Carman Neustaedter and Elena Fedorovskaya, "Presenting Identity in a Virtual World through Avatar Appearances," in *Proceedings of Graphics Interface 2009* (Canadian Information Processing Society, 2009), 183–190, http://dl.acm.org/citation.cfm?id=1555921.

[10] Paul R. Messinger et al., "On the Relationship between My Avatar and Myself," *Journal For Virtual Worlds Research* 1, no. 2 (2008), https://jvwr-ojs-utexas.tdl.org/jvwr/index.php/jvwr/article/view/352.

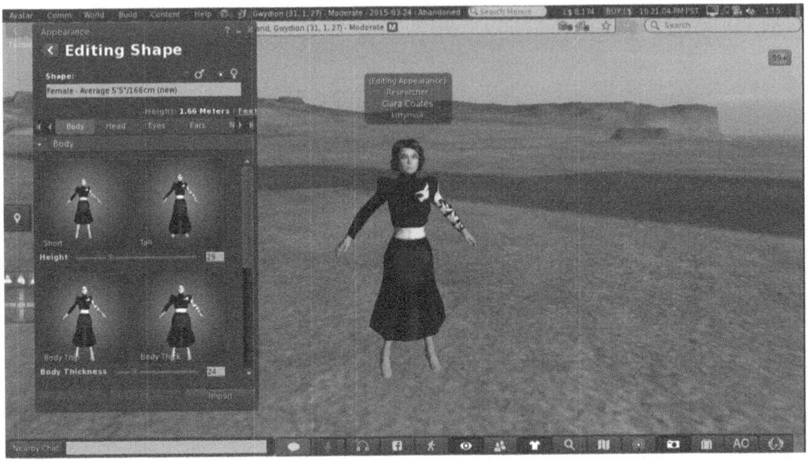

Fig. 3.2 Editing an avatar in SL

using the avatar to recreate a replica of their offline selves including through uploading an image of their physical face to a programme which will create a new face for their avatar.[11] This is, however, an uncommon practice, with most users choosing an approximation from those avatars which are readily available or using customising tools to construct their own (Fig. 3.2). This emphasis on presenting a "real" or "true" face is indicative of the messy relationship between the notion of the body and of the avatar as true repositories of self.

The importance of avatars to interaction in SL is emphasised by the tendency of residents to engage in "virtual makeovers" where a fellow resident does not meet the appearance standards of a group.[12] During the period of our research, Clara Coates decided to spend time with the tiny community. Her avatar, a human female, did not fit in with the group culture. While the group did not exclude her because of her avatar appearance, they were encouraging when she expressed interest in constructing a tiny persona. When she told a member of this group that she did not know where to purchase a tiny avatar, she was escorted by a group of five tinies to a popular shop. Here her new friends offered suggestions on the

[11] Geraldine F. Bloustien and Denise Wood, "Face, Authenticity, Transformations and Aesthetics in Second Life," *Body & Society* 19, no. 1 (March 2013): 52–81, https://doi.org/10.1177/1357034X12462250.

[12] Neustaedter and Fedorovskaya, "Presenting Identity in a Virtual World through Avatar Appearances."

form she should take. When she purchased and tried on her new avatar, they provided her with multiple outfits and a range of animations and expressions which would enable her to participate fully in the new community. The most notable of these was the "riverdance" expression, which is used whenever tinies celebrate together. Clara Coates, along with the group, performed this expression to celebrate her makeover. Here the makeover, and subsequent celebration, took the form of an informal ceremony through which Clara Coates was welcomed into a new community. While the process appeared unplanned, the makeover attracted a large group of tiny residents, all of whom contributed to the transformation and offered advice and suggestions. In contrast, when Clara Coates took MargieG to purchase her own tiny avatar, the lack of other community members made the makeover feel less like a ceremony than a transaction. The end result, however, was the same—both Clara Coates as a squirrel and MargieG as a husky are able to pass unnoticed in events hosted by the tiny community. The ceremony was thus not an integral part of becoming a tiny, but it served as an introduction and a welcome to that community. It was also a means of imparting essential cultural knowledge such as an understanding of the purpose of the "riverdance" expression.

For some residents, finding an appropriate avatar is not a simple task. While it is possible to take almost any form in SL, a resident without skills in graphic design or building is most likely to be reliant on adapting the default shape through the editing menu or purchasing a desired form. This latter approach provides many options—it is possible to buy full avatars or constituent body parts. There are countless tattoos, faces, and bodies available. Even outside of human avatars, it is possible to purchase a wide array of animal or object shapes. Notably absent from this vast marketplace, however, are avatars which portray a realistic human body marked by age. One of our interviewees, Meredith, works with older people and assists them in using SL. While many of the residents Meredith works with are comfortable with the default avatars, others find it difficult to find an appearance that fits their perception of self. She said:

> [One resident] was distressed that he looked too young. He wanted to find a different look. He ended up as a bird because he couldn't find the right human look. [...] He wanted to be an older—not old—man.

The ageless avatar body, then, leaves out those who do not see themselves represented in these idealised images of youth. These residents cannot create the "truthful" representation of the physical self which characterises so many avatar choices. This experience, and the compromise the resident made by choosing to represent himself as a bird, demonstrates a disconnect between avatar norms and the way in which some residents choose to represent themselves. Meredith stated that this resident was known for his rich, clear voice and that it was only when he became aware that others noticed his voice more than his avatar embodiment that he became comfortable with his SL appearance. The fact that he was able to obtain a non-human avatar which better suited his needs suggests that even residents who do not possess technical skills are to some extent able to move beyond the ageless human avatar norm. The norm, however, is unchangeable. Even fantastic creatures present within SL take a humanoid form—trolls or vampires retain a human shape. Furries, members of a subculture which privileges animal representations, are distinguishable due to the anthropomorphic nature of these animal embodiments. The only recognisable subculture we have encountered which regularly and entirely eschews human norms are the tinies, whose animal representations often nevertheless walk on hindquarters and wear clothes. To represent oneself as a small bird is therefore a radical act in the context of SL.

The human embodiment of SL residents is almost invariably white embodiment. The politics of representation in virtual worlds and MMORPGs has been examined fruitfully, including by Higgin who has described the tendency of games set in fantasy worlds to erase or obscure blackness and present humanity as predominantly European as "blackless fantasy."[13] In SL, where the potential forms of embodiment available are theoretically limitless, the relative absence of black bodies in particular, but other non-white bodies more broadly, is a visible corporeal hierarchy of value. Indeed, it has been posited that residents generally choose forms of embodiment that they believe are likely to be socially acceptable.[14] Some research has suggested that, where black residents enter less diverse virtual spaces, they are less likely to reveal their offline racial identity and more likely to choose white avatars.[15] Virtual diversity, in this sense, may

[13] "Blackless Fantasy: The Disappearance of Race in Massively Multiplayer Online Role-Playing Games," *Games and Culture* 4, no. 1 (December 1, 2008): 3–26, https://doi.org/10.1177/1555412008325477.

[14] Rosa Mikeal Martey and Mia Consalvo, "Performing the Looking-Glass Self: Avatar Appearance and Group Identity in Second Life," *Popular Communication* 9, no. 3 (July 1, 2011): 165–80, https://doi.org/10.1080/15405702.2011.583830.

[15] Jong-Eun Roselyn Lee, "Does Virtual Diversity Matter?: Effects of Avatar-Based Diversity Representation on Willingness to Express Offline Racial Identity and Avatar

help to provide a space for more "true" representations of the offline identities of marginalised groups. The predominantly white avatars of SL may, correspondingly, encourage "virtual passing." In the course of our fieldwork we have not encountered any discussions about race, nor did we initiate such conversations. We are ourselves both white women using white avatars. Our own representation and position have potentially closed off an important avenue of inquiry. We cannot, therefore, make any conclusions about the impact of the relative lack of visual diversity in SL on the connectedness of residents who are not white.

Second Lives as Real Lives

Despite the difficulties some residents face in developing appropriate avatar forms, those who choose to interact and form relationships in SL do so as embodied selves in a three-dimensional world. The reality of the lives lived within virtual worlds is the subject of debate. Velleman holds that, where residents "do" things in the virtual world, they are in fact using their real autonomy in order to perform fictional actions.[16] That is, they are really performing the actions performed by their avatar. He states that a resident is "speaking the literal truth when he says of his avatar, 'This is me.'"[17] However, the me-ness of the avatar is associated with a user's level of comfort and capacity in relation to using the digital interface. A person who must think about the correct key to press in order to move forward or fly does not feel the same connection to their avatar as one who can perform an action without thinking about the mechanism through which that action is performed. From this perspective, the avatar is or can become the extension of the human body, a fictional creation performing fictional actions in a fictional world but which, for experienced users, performs these actions automatically, responding to thought just as the human body does. Velleman's view defends residents against charges of playing make-believe when identifying with the avatar. He indicates that all humans, whether they engage with virtual worlds or not, use one form of avatar—the physical body. For those who have to relearn the operation of the body, such as after a serious injury,

Customization," *Computers in Human Behavior* 36 (July 2014): 190–97, https://doi.org/10.1016/j.chb.2014.03.040.

[16] "Bodies, Selves," *American Imago* 65, no. 3 (2006): 405–26.

[17] Velleman, 407.

the very taken-for-grantedness of the body as an extension of self comes undone. The body, just as the avatar of an experienced user of virtual worlds, seems to respond to intentions without the need to proactively command it to follow instructions. It is easy to forget the slow and painful process of learning to operate this physical avatar during infancy and early childhood. The body is a means through which the self as thinker and intender is able to act upon the world. For Velleman actions performed in the physical world are often—but not always—real actions really performed by the actor. Actions performed by avatars are often—but again not always—fictional actions, really performed.

All of these actions are indeed really performed in that the thinking self acts upon the world, virtual or physical, through the relevant avatar. In SL, the reality of the actions performed by the avatar and the connection of self to avatar are influenced by the way in which the resident understands SL. If they view it as a real place, then Velleman's fictional actions, really performed, become in fact real actions, really performed. Where a resident has become a moral actor through the development of the digital flesh, most of their actions in SL are indeed real actions, really performed, with a similar moral impact to those performed through the avatar of the body. However, this is a contested notion. While most long-term residents would agree that their lives in SL have meaning, not all would agree that SL is real or that the actions they perform within SL are real actions. This in turn can set up complex ideas around thresholds of grievability and when, where, or how a life that is formed with others constitutes a grievable life.

Some of our interviewees clearly subscribed to the notion that SL is fictional. One resident, who only uses SL as an extension of his offline job, told us that SL should not be seen as separate from other parts of life. He specifically railed against the idea that SL identities could be separated from other aspects of a person's identity. "The idea that you can be one person in SL and a different person in RL is a dangerous delusion," he told us. For him, a life lived in SL was valuable and grievable only as part of a richer, "real" life lived offline. SL was a space for working, playing, and having fun—it was not a place in which a life could be formed. For residents with this perspective, the very idea that SL could be anything other than a fictional space was dangerous. Such an ethos not only prevents the construction of the digital flesh but actively serves to encourage an active disregard of the digital flesh of others. It is not, however, an amoral position or one which suggests that no moral harm can occur in SL. Instead, it is one that accords residents a moral status relating to their status as physically embodied humans rather than digitally embodied avatars.

However, this was an uncommon perspective in the course of our research. Based on our observations and conversations with interviewees, we argue that lives are formed in SL through routine engagement, through the formation of complex and meaningful social relations such as those described in the previous chapter, and through engaging in tasks and activities which are meaningful to the residents themselves. These residents *really* do the things their avatars do and *really* form the relationships their avatars form. While we do not state that SL lives are equivalent to lives lived offline—such an argument would be difficult to support—this does not mean that they are not *real*. As one resident put it:

> In SL, we refer to ourselves as "residents." We understand that SL is simply another facet of our lives. A Second Life, to be sure. But important in its own right.

The same resident told us that the loss of a person known only as an avatar hurts in the same way as the loss of someone known through physical interactions. For him, the fact that a person who was part of one's daily routine is suddenly absent is no less devastating because they were known only as an avatar. This was a sentiment shared by many of the residents we spoke to. However, a key theme of our interviews was a sense that some (other) residents forget that they talk to real people when they interact on SL. One resident, Jane, said that:

> People can harm the emotions of others sometimes in how they treat people. I've seen people become so deflated. Not sure what they gain by that. Hurting the feelings of others. In RL that would not happen so easily as it does here.

A common way of putting it was that these residents "forget there's a person behind the screen." This is an idea that privileges the non-avatar self. The digital self is valued primarily as an extension of the physical, clearly grievable, self. There is a tension, then, between those who view SL as real, who see relationships formed in SL as valuable, and who mourn the loss of these relationships when they pass, and those who view SL as a game in which their own actions matter little. We did not speak to many members of this latter group, but their influence over the lives of more seriously embedded residents was evident in many stories of manipulation, deceit, and betrayal. These narratives speak to the competing notions of the real which can be accepted simultaneously in relation to SL. However, cruelty and unkindness occur because the real (physical) people operating avatars are obscured by the (presumably fictional) nature of avatars themselves. The flesh-and-blood self is held out in these narratives as a reason to respect the digital self. The digital flesh is therefore vulnerable and, correspondingly, grievable, because it is tethered to the soft, vulnerable flesh of the physically embodied self.

These different ways of understanding correct behaviour in the context of online relationships point to a disparity in understandings of moral personhood. The question of what it means to be granted moral status as a person—a person with a meaningful life—is a complicated one. In answering it, there is a risk of "perform[ing] normative violence [...] precisely through the closure and finitude involved in the delineation of qualifying conditions of 'the human' or 'person.'"[18] Those residents who act as though they are playing a game appear to exclude SL avatars from holding the status of "person," enabling them to act according to their own inclinations with no concern for how this may impact other residents. If SL is a game and residents are merely players, then the actions one performs therein have limited or no moral meaning. Such a position is in contrast with that taken by the many residents who have formed meaningful relationships and, indeed, lost and grieved such relationships in SL.

The narratives of residents we spoke to highlight the need to differentiate between offline identities and SL identities. One resident highlighted the degree of choice available when forming SL identities. He said:

> SL gives you an opportunity to reinvent yourself if you want. You can come here and be "you" or you can be somebody totally different, or you can be a variant of "you."

Another resident, Aida, describes living in SL as enabling her to fulfil her real dreams. She states that she has always wanted to be a radio personality. In SL she is able to work as a DJ. She enjoys the responses to her work and feels satisfied when other residents say that she should work in radio in her real life. She states that "Everyone would LOVE to live like SL." She also told us that her avatar, while not looking like her, reflects her true personality. As such, she believed that her friends and fans knew the "real" her. In this case the "real" self was an idealised self which was not

[18] Ashley Taylor, "'Lives Worth Living:' Theorizing Moral Status and Expressions of Human Life," *Disability Studies Quarterly* 33, no. 4 (September 5, 2013), http://dsq-sds.org/article/view/3875.

possible in a physical environment but which Aida viewed as more authentic than an embodied self which did not live up to her self-image. By removing herself from the constraints associated with physical presence which is so determined by class and biology, she was able to present a version of self which she understood as more authentic. In this sense some residents come to view SL as a space in which they are more real than they are in physical "reality."

These diverse perspectives demonstrate that there is no simple dichotomy between "real" offline self and "unreal" avatar self. Equally, however, they indicate that it is not enough to describe the avatar simply as an extension of the offline self. The avatar is able to do more and is often able to live in a manner that would be unobtainable offline. Previous research has shown that residents of SL are able to meet some needs, such as the need to socialise, in SL more fully than is possible in the offline world.[19] This further complicates the relationship between offline and online self, indicating that the needs of a person may be met through the alternative life of their avatar. The avatar self and embodied self are therefore two distinct, but interconnected, entities. The avatar cannot exist without the embodied self, but in some cases the needs of the embodied self cannot be met without the avatar. This highlights the continuing problem of the notion of a "true" self in a computer-mediated world. It also speaks to the science fiction ideals of death denial associated with computers insofar as the idea that the "true" self is distinct from the physical flesh is at the heart of mind-uploading fantasies. If the "true" self is the thinking, feeling, intellectual self, then the reality of avatar lives becomes incontestable. However, if the "true" self is rooted in our embodied realities—the sum of our physical body, our physical experiences, and our social and geographic location alongside our thinking, feeling, and intellectual qualities—then the avatar is a mere representation. Whatever the place of the body in the development of a "true" self, it is undeniable that residents seek to construct idealised lives within SL and that at times they position these lives as more "true" to their individual identity than the embodied lives they are experiencing.

Living as a "true" self in SL can involve replicating embodied rites of passage. There is a clear desire on the part of many residents to re-enact

[19] Timo Partala, "Psychological Needs and Virtual Worlds: Case Second Life," *International Journal of Human-Computer Studies* 69, no. 12 (December 2011): 787–800, https://doi.org/10.1016/j.ijhcs.2011.07.004.

aspects of their offline lives—or aspects of the offline lives of others—within SL. One example is virtual pregnancies. Based on our own conversations, we believe that people who choose to become pregnant in SL are largely women who are mothers offline. They are therefore not seeking to experience something which is otherwise closed to them but re-enacting their own embodied memories. By re-enacting, we mean that they engage in performative repetitions which do not recuperate past experiences in a magical self-identical way but in fact open up the experience of understanding that the past cannot be replicated. Virtual children have been explored in the previous chapter; however, no detailed description has so far been offered of the experience of virtual pregnancy itself. There is a thriving industry dedicated to allowing avatars in SL to become pregnant.[20] In our fieldwork we have come across a few variations of this theme. Some locations are simply retail facilities. It is possible to purchase animated babies or children and, if one desires, to purchase an attachment which will make one's avatar appear to be pregnant. At the opposite end of the spectrum is a fertility clinic. An avatar is required to attach a pregnancy belly, but this in itself does not make them pregnant. Instead, they must be artificially inseminated. The clinic even allows male residents to take on the role of "donating sperm" in order to create virtual children. Once the period of pregnancy is over, residents must return to the clinic to give birth. They then have the option of purchasing their baby or leaving it to be "adopted" by another resident. This presents an interesting ethical quandary in that a resident who is dissatisfied with the appearance of their baby, or who is unable to pay for it, must or may leave it to be adopted by an unknown family. It also raises the question of who is doing the adopting given that this fertility clinic advertises itself as a space in which avatars can become pregnant, rather than one in which avatars can adopt children, and also given the prevalence of spaces specifically tailored to allow the adoption of children.

Ellie, whose blended family was examined in the previous chapter, chose to undergo pregnancy through the use of the popular Zooby pregnancy attachment. These attachments are available in retail stores and on the SL marketplace. This is the most popular form of avatar pregnancy and is not as invasive as those that require artificial insemination. Other forms of pregnancy are more clearly connected to the medical industry in SL. In one

[20] Anna M. Lomanowska and Matthieu J. Guitton, "My Avatar Is Pregnant! Representation of Pregnancy, Birth, and Maternity in a Virtual World," *Computers in Human Behavior* 31 (February 2014): 322–31, https://doi.org/10.1016/j.chb.2013.10.058.

medical centre we encountered an automatic abortion machine—something which is perhaps implied by the medicalised pregnancy model in some such centres but which is unnecessary given that simply removing the relevant attachment can end a pregnancy. We have not encountered any residents who have made use of such a device, and indeed it may exist as a type of joke or commentary on the possibility of replicating pregnancies in SL.

Other attempts to re-enact aspects of the offline world occur in the realm of business. This is in itself a selling point of SL, and much of the early media hype focused on success stories. The most famous of these SL successes is Anshe Chung, a virtual real estate developer who was hailed as the "first virtual millionaire."[21] This early stage of SL's history was also characterised by the development of digital headquarters for global brands. Most of these brands have now disappeared, and major SL business success stories are today almost unheard of.

This has not prevented residents from engaging in commerce. Outside of our own interviewees, there are residents who invest significant amounts of time into running SL businesses. In particular, there are a number of fashion designers who own multiple shopfronts and release new items on almost a daily basis. The most seemingly successful of these designers are those who cater to a specific niche clientele. One designer, Sonetta Morales,[22] has shopfronts in 1920s Berlin (discussed in Chap. 6, *Nostalgia*) and 1920s Chicago, a sim owned by the same creator. Her luxurious historically accurate clothing is a common sight in these sims. It is in a sense a marker of class, taste, and community knowledge. Her ability to co-opt histories and designs associated with physical bodies and adopt them to the needs and desires of a virtual population is at the heart of her success. Thus her stores speak to the relevance of the ideas of authenticity and true history in an environment in which the nature of reality and what constitutes a real life is contested and altered.

Erik told us that he entered SL initially because he heard that offline businesses were creating shopfronts in SL. He saw this as a potential opportunity:

> At the end of 2006 I heard that a bank opened an office. A RL bank. And I thought …. Maybe I can start a RL business here also. I'm an antique dealer in RL. So I thought I could open a shop here and sell RL antiques. But that

[21] "Ansche Chung: First Virtual Millionaire," *CNN Money*, November 27, 2006, http://money.cnn.com/blogs/legalpad/2006/11/anshe-chung-first-virtual-millionaire.html.

[22] We did not interview Sonetta Morales. We use her real avatar name as she is a public figure in SL.

> didn't really work out because I liked to roleplay more. So I started [role-playing] and forgot the RL business.

Erik has created an intricate and evocative sim used for vampire roleplay. At the centre is a cathedral, modelled after one he has visited many times in Amiens, France. He built a city around the church. "This is my dream world," he said, "I created it." Here Erik alludes to the opening up of possibilities in SL. Within this context it is possible for residents to enact grand designs. They can be town planners or architects. The gatekeepers which serve as barriers to creation offline are removed, allowing people like Erik to literally become the architects of their own reality. The value of SL for him was not in its ability to extend and replicate the "real" but to offer a reality which was more malleable and offered greater potential for self-actualisation. Erik role-plays as a vampire lord in an environment he has created for himself. His work attracts like-minded people who become close friends and confidants, known and knowable both as role-play characters and friends outside of their prescribed roles. The transition from hopeful entrepreneur to vampire lord was thus associated with a shift in values and understandings, which allowed a new interpretation of reality in relation to virtual worlds. The forms of play and relationships possible in SL have come to outweigh any imagined financial opportunities.

Digital lives encompass more than friendship, play, and commerce. Other aspects of the offline world have found their way into SL. Jerome Newstart[23] is the minister of the First United Church of Christ, Second Life. This is an accredited digital campus of the real US Christian denomination. He initiated the creation of the church "to provide access to worship and community (latter very important) for marginalised groups in particular." He states that his role is in some ways very similar to that he performs offline—he leads worship on a regular basis. However, he describes himself as "more of a community organiser in SL than I had ever been in RL." He has worked to create a safe space for residents in SL. He said that:

> By 'church' I mean a progressive form of Christianity that believes in offering an extravagant welcome as I like to call it. [...] Jesus did not reject; we don't either. Many of our folks are LGBTQIA. Others are physically impaired or have such things as panic disorder. Others are not so challenged.

[23] Jerome Newstart's real avatar name is used here as he is easily identifiable.

Jerome's description of his work demonstrates that he has adapted his ministry in order to meet the needs of the SL community. He remains aware of the specific needs of this population, which, as he notes, includes people who may have faced rejection or marginalisation elsewhere. It is difficult to ascertain the number of residents who attend worship services, at Jerome's church or any other religious institution, on a regular basis. However, when we visited we found groups of six or seven attendees at Saturday psalter events and around double that at the Sunday service. This, along with the fact that the First United Church of Christ, Second Life and other religious institutions are able to continue existing, suggests that there is a group of residents who are comfortable having their spiritual needs met within the SL context.

Others have indicated that SL is a space in which their intellectual needs are met. Kai Woodhouse described his first impressions of SL:

> The experience of being in Second Life can be a bit like going to a museum ... or an amusement park say .... At first it is cool going around seeing things ... but by the afternoon you start to get museum'd out (or amusement park'd out, as the case may be). That is, fatigue starts to set in.

From Kai's perspective, it is when fatigue sets in that one either chooses to develop a real life in SL or leave. When Kai himself became less interested in exploring SL, he decided to stay in part because he enjoyed owning his own homes and, in part, because he quickly became part of a community based around discussion events. His favourite group was called Socrates Café. This was "a kind of group discussion where people get together to talk about ... whatever kind of philosophical topic comes up in a session." He believed that such groups worked particularly well in SL as the fact that users were represented by avatars rather than physically embodied and could participate via text reduced barriers to participation. Kai, who has a postgraduate history degree, said that discussions in SL allowed him to recapture some of the experience of attending academic seminars and bouncing ideas off fellow students. He eventually began to lead other discussion groups, some focusing on philosophy, others centred on history or current affairs.

The type of serious discussion and consideration which can be found in SL is perhaps demonstrated most clearly by an annual event. On February 5, 2017, the annual World Religion Day event, which attracted 50 residents, included representatives from ten faith groups speaking on the subject “The Spiritual Foundations of World Peace.” The fact that an interfaith discussion event can attract a large crowd and continue to do so each year speaks to a population which is interested in a deep engagement with one another and with challenging ideas. If we were to position SL as nothing more than a “game,” the presence of these very serious and important events would be difficult to explain. While these are clearly a source of enjoyment and satisfaction to residents, they do not fit within existing popular discourses relating to games.

While Kai described the possibility of being “museum’d out,” other residents view SL as a space in which they can create high-quality, immersive museum experiences on a low budget. Takashi runs a museum dedicated to nuclear warfare. Offline, he has expertise in museum curation and has written a graduate thesis on warships as museum exhibits. After witnessing the constraints placed upon small museums by such factors as finance and physical space, he was inspired to use SL as a space in which to experiment with new forms of presentation.

> You can probably guess that it would not be possible to showcase over 130 megatons worth of nuclear ordinance to the public in RL. [...] It would take millions of dollars and a huge legal process to build something like this in RL, but here we dispense with that.

Takashi has a large inventory which allows him to rotate exhibitions on a regular basis. In keeping with his expertise, he focuses on displaying large-scale vehicles and weapons. While similar items can be purchased readily on the Second Life Marketplace, Takashi has found that these are invariable historically inaccurate. The items he displays are the result of a merger between his historical research skills and the building talents of friends. In addition to showing the items, he provides Wikipedia links both to articles about the historical artefacts themselves and to pop culture properties which have reinterpreted these items. In merging traditional museum-style displays with the type of information trail only possible online, Takashi has constructed a museum that is recognisable as such while taking full advantage of the opportunities SL offers. He sees his work in the museum as real, if unpaid, work and SL as a possible future for small-scale museums. In a sense Takashi’s work demonstrates both the presence of serious and informative activities in SL and the possibility of residents engaging in lives that are more “real” than their “real” lives within SL. Takashi would be unable to build a museum of the scale he has constructed in SL anywhere else. He is in the process of seeking tax-exempt status for his in-world museum, demonstrating that he believes his work is true heritage work which should be recognised offline and in official documentation. Takashi has a diagnosis of autism. He finds that SL allows him to pursue his work while remaining in control of the circumstances in which he comes into contact with others. His narrative is thus one in which personal, physical, and financial barriers have been surpassed, allowing him to create a truly immersive and creative educational space.

There is also a strong charity sector in SL. Isabelle works in-world as a fundraiser. Her father died of Parkinson's disease, and her mother was diagnosed with the same illness a year later. While Isabelle's narrative of her SL experiences is described more fully in a later chapter, here we would like to briefly acknowledge the fundraising work she does. She runs a sim which features a range of performing spaces, all of which are used to host charity benefits for the aid of the Michael J. Fox Foundation. Her sim also hosts an array of shops, all of which donate 50% of all profits to the same foundation. Isabelle is extremely successful in her fundraising work and has been recognised for this work offline. The work she does in SL has an undeniable "real" impact on people living with the embodied reality of Parkinson's disease. Isabelle is far from the only significant fundraiser in-world.

Perhaps the best evidence that lives lived in SL are, in fact, real lives, is found in the everyday pleasures people enjoy in SL. Laura, whose relationship with Elliott was described in the previous chapter, is not only an art gallery curator but also a SL photographer. She runs a blog featuring images which combine to provide a sense of her life in SL. These are sometimes highly stylised images featuring her own avatar in various forms and places. Other images are portraits of residents who are important to her. Elliott is featured in many of the more artistic photographs. On her blog she takes photographs of art shows, of notable figures, and of the places she explores. Her blog provides insight into the thriving SL art scene, which has its own cast of notable and known figures and an active calendar of events and shows. Ellie, on the other hand, has created an open children's garden. On this land, families with Zooby babies are free to come and play. The space is not entirely child-centric—it is designed as a safe place in which babies are able to roam and play with toys, while their mothers can spend time together, playing board games and socialising. Both Laura and Ellie spend enough time in SL that it is not a hobby in itself—it is a space in which one finds and develops hobbies and other pleasures.

It is important to note that, for the residents we have spoken to, SL lives, while real, are overwhelmingly understood as less important than lives lived offline. A few residents have spoken about addiction—a sense that people can become too invested in their SL experiences, to the detriment of their lives offline. This demonstrates the extent to which SL residents are embedded in prevalent discourses pathologising virtual worlds and those who engage with them. This is viewed as particularly problematic where SL relationships take over from those formed offline. However, interviewees have suggested other causes of addiction. One stated that roleplaying in SL was too immersive—in short, too real—and made him feel less engaged in his offline life. The digital flesh therefore becomes perceived as a liability where it becomes more tangible, more embedded in social connections and meaning, than the physical. The privileging of firstness over secondness and the enduring power of these categories render those deeply embedded in what ought to be their second life a threat or concern.

Disability and Illness in Second Life

The potential of SL as a space in which people with disabilities can form supportive communities has been a focus of existing research.[24] Best and Butler, for instance, created a space for social support for people with myalgic encephalomyelitis/chronic fatigue syndrome (ME/CFS) in SL. Their work highlighted both the possibilities of SL to promote such a space and the need to be mindful of accessibility in designing virtual environments. Their support centre, initially created without a knowledge of the impact of the virtual environment on symptoms, had to be redesigned after feedback from residents.[25] They also identified issues with avatar use, such as some residents living with ME/CFS finding that avatar use made them feel dizzy or nauseated or being unable to move their avatar through SL environments.[26] However, some residents found that they were able to

[24] E.g. Karen Stendal, Susan Balandin, and Judith Molka-Danielsen, "Virtual Worlds: A New Opportunity for People with Lifelong Disability?," *Journal of Intellectual and Developmental Disability* 36, no. 1 (March 2011): 80–83, https://doi.org/10.3109/13668250.2011.526597.

[25] "Virtual Space: Creating a Place for Social Support in Second Life," *Space and Culture* 18, no. 2 (May 2015): 194, https://doi.org/10.1177/1206331213512235.

[26] Kirsty Best and Stephanie Butler, "Second Life Avatars as Extensions of Social and Physical Bodies in People with Myalgic Encephalomyelitis/Chronic Fatigue Syndrome,"

"closet" their illness in SL and engage in social interaction without the stigma attached to living with ME/CFS.[27]

In our own fieldwork, we met residents who were engaged in connecting and supporting people with health concerns. Meredith runs a sim in which she assists older people in accessing SL and provides a range of health and wellness programmes. She and her husband created a registered non-profit organisation through which the sim is run. Meredith told us that, in the past year, she has received assistance from a professor at a local university, who has encouraged students to aid her in encouraging and teaching older people to use SL. She has already hired one student whom she met through this programme and hopes to receive a steady stream of volunteers. Currently, she funds the work herself from her income as a professional therapist. In the future, she hopes to find outside funding. However, for this to occur, she will need to articulate a case for the value of engagement with SL. This will require an ability to overcome the existing limiting discursive constructions of virtual worlds as unserious or dangerous.

Meredith has found that many of the older people who use her sim have entered SL because they are experiencing a lack of intellectual engagement and companionship in their offline lives. Others come looking for new experiences. She said of one resident:

> [He] lives in subsidised housing and barely has a computer. He has made friends in SL and is quite well known but he lives a pretty isolated real life. Here he writes poetry and plays live music.

Demographics of real-life illness, disability, and socio-economic disadvantage, and other factors that limit access to intelligent conversation, creativity, sexuality, and fun, are part of SL's social function and continuing survival. People with disabilities and poor health can live more freely in a place like SL and exercise agency about who they are in the dynamic self-recognition and perception through others. Such an idea necessarily privileges non-disabled bodies as well as the notion that an authentic life is one in which individuals are able to do as they please. There are also spaces for support with mental illness in SL. Carmine Thomas provides the funding for a support group for survivors of suicide. The group provides peer-to-peer support in SL for people

Continuum 27, no. 6 (December 2013): 841–42, https://doi.org/10.1080/10304312.2013.794190.

[27] Best and Butler, 843.

who have attempted suicide. They also provide volunteer mentors who help to monitor and moderate meetings. Carmine provides financial support for this group, not because he spends much time in SL himself but because "knowing that it was there has always been a bit of a comfort." He lives an isolated lifestyle offline, in part due to his working conditions and partly because he has a mental illness which makes it difficult to live near people. He states that there have been moments when he has needed to come online and speak to someone. At these times he contacts the group or its leader. "Knowing that someone is listening, has an idea of what I'm going through helps," he said. Other people living with mental illness find SL a space in which they can live on an equal basis with others. Chaos has schizoaffective disorder and PTSD. In her offline life, she is unable to work. In SL, she is able to devote her time to promoting inclusion for transgender people. Both Chaos and Carmine are able to use their own resources to support others in SL despite the varying constraints placed upon them by their mental illnesses. Thus SL has become for them a place in which they are able to offer support to others who may be experiencing similar health issues.

Other residents told us about friends with disabilities or chronic illnesses. Erik states that "sickness and disability rule over SL." He clarifies that a large proportion of his friends are disabled or seriously ill and "I can't believe only my friends have it." In particular, he described a good friend who is physically paralysed. In SL, he said, his friend is an active and respected roleplayer who "drives women nuts." Here he hints at a belief that his friend may be unable to find romantic partners offline. However, the ability to overcome physical limitations is not the only benefit of engagement in SL for people with disability and long-term illnesses.

Support at times extends to practical and financial support. Jane told us about a network of close friends, two of whom, Kay and Alice, died of cancer a year apart. Both were in their 40s; Kay lived in Kentucky and was too ill to work for a long period leading up to her death. Jane, who had connected with Kay on Facebook and elsewhere outside of SL, paid for Kay's phone bill during the last six months of her life as her insurance would not cover it. When Kay's brothers, who did not support her leading up to her death, did not organise a funeral, Jane and her SL friends joined together to raise funds for a proper send-off. A single resident donated $1000 USD. In total, they were able to raise $1800 which was sent to Kay's roommate for the funeral.

Jane, who is a long-term resident of SL and has worked as a volunteer "helper" for new residents, told us that many of her friends in SL had illnesses offline. In many cases, these illnesses impeded their mobility. She described another friend, Vincent, who died at the age of 42 from a brain tumour. Vincent was "basically a clown," a fun person who liked to spend time at Help Island, an orientation island, providing support. Jane's long-term engagement with Help Island appears to be the source of many friendships with people who have been ill or who have passed away.

For those residents who have lost long-term friends to illness, there is a sense that lives in SL are inherently fragile. There is also a sense that they are valuable—both residents with illness or disability and their friends told us that SL is a space in which it is possible to overcome physical limitations and feel free. For those with mental illnesses, it is a space in which interaction can occur at one's own pace—where one can halt a conversation by walking away from the keyboard or logging off and where one can take complete control over embodiment and self-representation. All of this renders SL lives particularly valuable as a space for working, travelling, and forming relationships. Some residents have suggested that, for people who are limited by disability or other marginalising factors, life in SL is more "real" than reality.

Remembering Grievable Lives

The next chapter will explore the commemorative culture of SL. Here we provide a brief discussion of the ways in which mourning occurs and the way in which this mourning speaks to our argument that SL lives are grievable lives. We also detail some of the more idiosyncratic forms of mourning which suggest the creative responses of residents to the loss of SL loved ones. We argue that the mourning practices we witness in SL are not only a response to the loss of the life "behind the keyboard"—the human life which makes the life of the avatar possible—but also a response to the loss of the avatar life itself.

Offline, those who lose a loved one find themselves enmeshed in established rituals which perpetuate and solidify existing hierarchies of grief. Butler points to the obituary as a means of legitimating grief and demonstrating that a life is indeed grievable. She states that norms govern which lives can be legitimised in this way and also which lives cannot be publically grieved.[28] Our research has shown that these norms—norms relating

[28] Butler, "Violence, Mourning, Politics," 25.

to who can dictate the way in which a life is mourned and who can in fact be mourned—are understood differently within SL. A few examples serve to demonstrate the way in which this occurs.

The Countess, an impossibly glamorous figure with a glowing avatar, wrote a book after the passage of her SL lover. The Countess speaks in Italian, using a translation app in order to communicate with English-speaking SL residents. Her book is also written in the Italian language and has been translated for us by our colleague at Griffith University, Claire Kennedy. In her book, The Countess writes the story of her relationship. She explains that, when she met her partner, his typing was slow "as if there was some effort on his part to respond." He was on bed rest at the time of their meeting and "lived here [SL]." She hints at a language barrier:

> It goes without saying that it was very hard work sharing the things that we decided together because communication was limited to confused words, both written and spoken, but despite this we intended to remain united.

The relationship is not described as having been perfect—The Countess states that he proposed through a video and that she "wasn't very convinced about it" but "accepted so as not to sadden him." Similarly, she states that:

> Time passed inexorably and being with him became increasingly oppressive, but despite the problems he gave me much love, in his own way sure, but it was clear that he was sincere and he truly loved me.

She describes him as having bad moods and complaining about his life. Eventually, she writes:

> I told him he had to stop being sorry for himself, that he had to fight and not give up [...], that I was sick of his complaining and that I too had my problems and didn't know what I could do for him anymore.
>
> I had a lump in my throat, I was barely holding back my tears, but I couldn't go on like that any longer.
>
> I told him I was going to leave, that I couldn't stay with him any longer, that if I had continued I would have got sick and I couldn't, didn't want to, allow this to happen.

This is a deeply embodied description of grief. The Countess was visible to her former partner only as avatar. He could not see her physical condition. Despite this, she describes holding back tears, as though she were trying to prevent him from seeing them. In this context, the barrier between avatar and self appears to have temporarily disintegrated.

Despite breaking up with her partner, she continued to keep in touch with him. She states that he went away from SL for a period of time so he could undertake an operation. When he returned, he seemed to be doing better. However, she states, he was soon in declining health. He told her that his life was going to end and soon afterwards disappeared. She writes that, on October 8, 2013, she gathered her friends and held a ceremony to say farewell.

The Countess's narrative speaks to a grief which would be disenfranchised elsewhere. Her partner did not speak the same language. She knew him only online and had broken up with him prior to his death. As Doka states,

> Even those whose relationships existed primarily in the past may experience grief. Ex-spouses, past lovers, or former friends may have limited contact or they may even engage in interaction in the present. Yet the death of that significant other can still cause a grief reaction because it brings finality to that earlier loss, ending any remaining contact or fantasy of reconciliation or reinvolvement.[29]

Such relationships, however, cannot always be publically grieved because there is no societal recognition that the loss of a relationship which has ended can be the source of grief. In SL, however, The Countess was able to memorialise her former partner with friends. She was also able to write and distribute a book based on her experiences, knowing that this would be accepted as a type of valid grief work in a space which celebrates creativity and authenticity.

Another resident, Erik, created a memorial in his vampire roleplaying sim. It became a popular space for memorialising people who had died offline, both SL users and their loved ones. He decided to create a memorial after losing friends to illness. He said:

> A lot of people forget that there are real people behind the avatar. There are a lot of assholes but also a nice of people. And it's bad .... But also a lot of sick people. People who are disabled in RL. People who have cancer.

[29] Kenneth J Doka, "Disenfranchised Grief," in *Disenfranchised Grief: Recognizing Hidden Sorrow*, ed. Kenneth J. Doka (Lexington, Mass: Lexington Books, 1989), 5.

He saw his memorial as a space in which the lives, marked and shortened by illness, of his own friends could be marked in a way that was personal and meaningful to those left behind. Many of the people Erik has memorialised died of cancer. Most memorials are accompanied by photographs of the deceased both in SL and offline. Many are very young. Erik told us the story of two lovers, both of whom had life-limiting illnesses. They met in SL and fell in love, making plans to marry offline. Before they could meet, one partner died. A year later, the other passed away. Erik memorialised them together, using images of them interacting as a couple in SL. Years after their deaths, friends continue to leave flowers at their memorial. Here, again, we find a relationship which may not be recognised offline—two people who have never met physically, however devoted they may be to one another, can rarely expect to be memorialised as a couple. In SL, however, where they shared their relationship, this form of memorialisation is comprehensible and acceptable.

In other cases, people wear grief upon their avatar bodies. One resident, Sergio, told us about his decision to memorialise his partner, Amos, who died by recreating his avatar as a symbol of mourning. Sergio spoke Spanish and used an automated translator. Through this he explained that his torso was tattooed with coloured circles, each of which represented an emotion. Green circles represented hope, while yellow represented grief and loneliness. These interlinking circles formed a chain which ended in a black heart which Sergio said represented his dead heart. Sergio had been in a relationship with Amos both inside and out of SL—they had lived too far away to live together, but they communicated on Skype, Facebook, and WhatsApp.

The grief following the loss of a friend, combined with the anonymity of SL, appears to have encouraged some users to pretend that they had passed away. Jane told us several wild stories about people who had lied about their gender, disability, or other aspects of their lives and then had faked their own death. These stories had come out in various ways, including through supposedly new residents entering the friendship networks of the resident who had passed away and acting suspiciously familiar. In other cases enough facts were known about a resident's offline identity that the fact that they had not died could be ascertained. Jane said that "one person I met here refuses to believe anyone has really died because of all the fakers they know of." The knowledge that some residents do fake their own deaths certainly has an impact on the perceived grievability of SL lives for those who have been hurt in the past. The fact that memorials are dispersed through the virtual world despite this tendency demonstrates that these lives are held to be valuable and grievable, even in the context of a lack of certainty.

The prevalence of disability and illness in SL throws the grievability of avatar lives into a new light. The evidence from our research suggests that, for some residents, SL is a safe space in which they are able to interact without the same impediments they face offline. It is difficult to ascertain how many people living in SL experience some kind of health issues or limitations offline. However, from the stories of our interviewees, we are led to believe that it is a high proportion. We are also drawn to the perspective that avatar lives are all the more vital and grievable because of the centrality they can gain in the lives of people who are marginalised outside of SL. In the next chapter, we explore the ways in which these lives are in fact grieved. We also examine the culture of commemorating major, mostly US-centric, events and milestones.

CHAPTER 4

Commemorative Culture

Introduction

MargieG experienced an intimate scene of mourning in SL in an unexpectedly poignant way in December of 2014. She visited the Second Afterlife Cemetery and encountered a woman mourning the death of her biological brother who had died only a week before. Without intending to intrude or interrupt, MargieG found herself bearing witness to a scene of immediate grieving. It was an uncanny encounter. Margaret, as the physically embodied typist behind MargieG, was herself in the midst of a process of mourning. Her own biological brother had died only a few weeks earlier. She writes:

> I had a brief chat in text and become aware that despite the seamless, emotional mask of avatar appearances the woman was sad and indeed crying. She had made a memorial to her brother in SL within a week and was sitting by his grave, looking at his photo on the memorial headstone. She sat for a long time, rubbing her legs and moving her head. I knew even as I looked on at a respectful distance, that this was grieving through an avatar embodiment.

Memorials, as Erika Doss writes, are "bodies of feeling, cultural entities whose social, cultural and political meanings are determined by the emotional states and needs of their audiences."[1] Doss explores the memorial

[1] Erika Doss, *Memorial Mania: Public Feeling in America* (Chicago and London: University of Chicago Press, 2010), 46.

M. Gibson, C. Carden, *Living and Dying in a Virtual World*,
Palgrave Macmillan Memory Studies,
https://doi.org/10.1007/978-3-319-76099-5_4

culture of the USA through the thesis of "memorial mania." This thesis identifies the devolution of official commemorative monuments and rituals from the province of the nation-state and its more localised geographies and rituals of public commemoration to include temporary and spontaneous memorials responding to a range of circumstances of death. It is a trend which is evident not only in the USA but in other, divergent, cultural, and geographical environments. In twenty-first-century global media and mobile culture, activities of commemoration are significantly diverse in terms of production, temporalities, ritual forms, emotional contents, and modes of participatory culture. Mass media culture has produced not just "memorial mania"[2] but the capacity to bear witness to public and intimate mourning as it unfolds in close and distant places through mobile media sharing.[3] While physical memorials can be sites of pilgrimage or what has been termed "dark tourism" where travelling to and from the memorial is part of the ritual and experience,[4] online memorial culture moves away from these time-space ritual attributes of journeying. In the Anglosphere, the cultural turn towards celebrating a life, and not only mourning a death, is another key part of the emotional repertoire of contemporary memorial culture, online and offline, particularly for those individuals whose lives and talents are seen as having shifted social consciousness or otherwise shaped a generation.

The rise of user-generated media culture has been central to forces of commemorative democratisation. This democratisation is necessarily uneven, and the same media culture, epitomised by platforms such as YouTube and Twitter, extends and exposes local and global fault lines of hegemonic subjects and circumstances of mourning and "memory capital."[5] Celebrities, such as actors or musicians, are now routinely

[2] Erika Doss, *The Emotional Life of Contemporary Public Memorials: Towards a Theory of Temporary Memorials* (Amsterdam: Amsterdam University Press, 2008); Doss, *Memorial Mania: Public Feeling in America*.

[3] Kathleen Cumiskey and Larissa Hjorth, *Haunting Hands: Mobile Media Practices and Loss* (New York: Oxford University Press, 2017).

[4] Nick Osbaldiston and Theresa Petray, "The Role of Horror and Dread in the Sacred Experience," *Tourist Studies* 11, no. 2 (August 1, 2011): 175–90, https://doi.org/10.1177/1468797611424955; Brigitte Sion, "Memorial Pilgrimage or Death Tourism? A Jewish Perspective," *Liturgy* 32, no. 3 (July 3, 2017): 23–28, https://doi.org/10.1080/0458063X.2017.1295720.

[5] Anna Reading, "The London Bombings: Mobile Witnessing, Mortal Bodies and Globital Time," *Memory Studies* 4, no. 3 (July 2011): 298–311, https://doi.org/10.1177/1750698011402672.

mourned on a massive scale enabled through digital technologies.[6] Popular culture is increasingly transnational, albeit US-centric, and the scale of transnational identification forged around loved figures and fictional characters is a powerful factor in mediated mourning and memorialisation in contemporary life. These figures have become key parts of individual and generational biographies, and their loss can have a profound, shared, impact. The faces we see or the names we read consistently throughout our lives, whether fictional or real, become real to us. They are storied lives which become part of our own, shared storied lives. We may think of the grief that a generation of readers felt upon the death of Dumbledore, a fictional character from the *Harry Potter* book series. This was a figure who had, in a sense, been part of the experience of growing up for a generation. It has been suggested that digital technologies enable a type of suspension of disbelief wherein the lost celebrity may be maintained as a popular and influential figure long after their physical death.[7] Dumbledore himself, despite never having really existed, continues to be a lively presence on social media and in meme culture, alongside other deceased fictional characters, including some from the same franchise.

Transnational grieving of celebrity deaths has become an important part of internet, meme, and viral media cultures. In 2016, the world mourned the loss of a slate of major, culture-defining Western celebrities including David Bowie, Carrie Fisher, Leonard Cohen, and Alan Rickman. The online response was a combination of grief, shock, and a certain dark humour expressed in the form of jokes and memes about the year 2016 itself.[8] These deaths mark the beginning of the loss, on a massive scale, of

[6] Tony Walter, "Angels Not Souls: Popular Religion in the Online Mourning for British Celebrity Jade Goody," *Religion* 41, no. 1 (March 1, 2011): 29–51, https://doi.org/10.1080/0048721X.2011.553138; Anu Harju, "Socially Shared Mourning: Construction and Consumption of Collective Memory," *New Review of Hypermedia and Multimedia* 21, no. 1–2 (April 3, 2015): 123–45, https://doi.org/10.1080/13614568.2014.983562; Elizabeth L. Cohen and Cynthia Hoffner, "Finding Meaning in a Celebrity's Death: The Relationship between Parasocial Attachment, Grief, and Sharing Educational Health Information Related to Robin Williams on Social Network Sites," *Computers in Human Behavior* 65 (December 2016): 643–50, https://doi.org/10.1016/j.chb.2016.06.042.

[7] Alexandra Sherlock, "Larger Than Life: Digital Resurrection and the Re-Enchantment of Society," *The Information Society* 29, no. 3 (May 1, 2013): 164–76, https://doi.org/10.1080/01972243.2013.777302.

[8] E.g. Stephanie Dube Dwilson, "2016 Celebrity Deaths: All the Memes You Need to See," *Heavy.com* (blog), December 28, 2016, http://heavy.com/social/2016/12/2016-celebrity-deaths-memes-tweets-reactions-dear2016-dear-me-before-after-80s-carrie-fisher-

a generation of cultural icons. Given the prevalence of discussion and mourning around the loss of these figures online, their presence in the memorial culture of SL is unsurprising.

The memorialisation of individuals who had no celebrity status has also moved online. A significant body of research has been focused on the growth of memorials on the internet and ways it has created new formations of sociality and bonds between the living and dead and forms of bereavement.[9] Indeed across a range of platforms and sites, strangers are coming together to share stories and to remember their loved loves where common threads between people might be the circumstances of a loss or a relationship of loss—a mother who has lost a child, a sister who has lost a brother, and so on. The algorithms that collate and collect commemorative acts on sites such as YouTube and other spaces in which ordinary people are able to disseminate their own narratives are central to the rise and normalisation of sociality between strangers in the non-face-to-face of intimate publics of mourning.[10] In the digital network, the dead have a more lively "restless" status in terms of algorithms of remembrance built into social media platforms and in terms of the unexpected acts of shared

george-michael-prince-funny-pics-rip-memorial-pictures/; Lisa Respers France, "2016 Celebrity Deaths: A Year of Great Loss," News and Entertainment, CNN, December 26, 2016, http://www.cnn.com/2016/12/22/entertainment/2016-celebrity-deaths/index.html.

[9] Avril Maddrell, "Online Memorials: The Virtual as the New Vernacular," *Bereavement Care* 31, no. 2 (2012): 46–54; P Roberts and L Vidal, "Perpetual Care in Cyberspace: A Portrait of Memorials on the Web," *OMEGA—Journal of Death and Dying* 40, no. 4 (2000): 521–45; Pamela Roberts, "Here Today and Cyberspace Tomorrow: Memorials and Bereavement Support on the Web," *Generations* 28, no. 2 (2004): 41–46; Lisa M Mitchell et al., "Death and Grief on-Line: Virtual Memorialisation and Changing Concepts of Childhood Death and Parental Bereavement on the Internet," *Health Sociology Review: The Journal of the Health Section of the Australian Sociological Association* 21, no. 4 (2012): 413–31; Alice Marwick and Nicole B. Ellison, "'There Isn't Wifi in Heaven!' Negotiating Visibility on Facebook Memorial Pages," *Journal of Broadcasting & Electronic Media* 56, no. 3 (July 2012): 378–400, https://doi.org/10.1080/08838151.2012.705197; Miriam Moss, "Grief on the Web," *OMEGA—Journal of Death and Dying* 49, no. 1 (August 2004): 77–81, https://doi.org/10.2190/CQTK-GF27-TN42-3CW3; Tony Walter et al., "Does the Internet Change How We Die and Mourn? Overview and Analysis," *OMEGA—Journal of Death and Dying* 64, no. 4 (June 2012): 275–302, https://doi.org/10.2190/OM.64.4.a.

[10] Margaret Gibson and Golie Talaie Kamalabad, "Archives of Sadness: Sharing Bereavement and Generating Emotional Exchange between Strangers on YouTube," in *Digital Intimate Publics & Social Media*, ed. Amy Dobson, Nicholas Carah, and Brady Robards (Palgrave, Forthcoming).

remembrance, death announcements, and other commemorative practices that are posted and shared.[11] Social media sites such as Myspace and Facebook have contributed to the development of these new relationships with the dead, providing spaces in which connections can be maintained and narratives about the deceased shared.[12]

SL is part of this broader digital culture of shared grief. It is a place in which trends towards digital memorialisation, continued digital connections to the known deceased, and grieving of public figures are all played out. This alone renders the commemorative culture of SL a worthy subject of research. However, the very fact that SL is a place, and that residents living within SL are embodied, means that commemoration in SL takes a slightly different form to that elsewhere online. Further, the possibilities offered by SL, including possibilities for creating and placing objects, mean that commemoration and grief in SL take a hybrid form. It is embodied, enacted, ritualised grief, but it has the fluidity, creativity, and the openness to serendipity offered by the digital. This presents its own challenges and opportunities.

The commemorative culture of SL necessarily shares much with other commemorative cultures. It involves the sometimes difficult interplay and tension between visible and heard histories of death, sacrifice, murder, and grief and "other" counter-histories less visible and often actively silenced and delegitimised as sources of social, moral, and political change. Commemoration is about keeping the memory of historically and socio-politically significant events and places of trauma, grief, and loss ritually and narratively alive—in living memory—against the vagaries of forgetting. Rituals calling for remembrance are paramount in histories of commemoration, particularly those that have acquired a sacred status or hegemonic status (or both), nationally and transnationally. This hegemonic and sacred status is not just linked to nationalism but hegemons of masculinity that silence and delegitimise women's histories and particularly trauma histories of rape and murder in the context of war. While state-sanctioned commemorative culture remains a powerful moral force

[11] Michael Arnold et al., *Death and Digital Media*. (Routledge, 2017); Margaret Gibson, "Automatic and Automated Mourning: Messengers of Death and Messages from the Dead," *Continuum* 29, no. 3 (May 4, 2015): 339–53, https://doi.org/10.1080/10304312.2015.1025369.

[12] B. Carroll and K. Landry, "Logging On and Letting Out: Using Online Social Networks to Grieve and to Mourn," *Bulletin of Science, Technology & Society* 30, no. 5 (October 1, 2010): 341–49, https://doi.org/10.1177/0270467610380006.

in the cultivation of nationalist sentiment and solidarity through myth, story, and ritual, public mourning and memorial culture is increasingly borderless, mobile, and shaped by a range of identity sources, circumstances of death, and subjects of loss. For example, the death of Michael Jackson reached global proportions of reaction and interest.[13] His death was not only mourned but his life celebrated in a range of commemorative practices around the world, many involving performances of his music and dance routines. Not surprisingly, Michael Jackson has a memorial presence in SL with a dedicated tribute group who celebrate his music and dance.

The concept of counter-publics is valuable in exploring the opening up of memorialisation to lives and social and trauma histories traditionally excluded from hegemonies of public mourning and memory ritual.[14] Commemorative counter-publics tend to "voice oppositional needs and values not by appealing to the universality of the bourgeois public sphere but by affirming specificity of race, gender, sexuality, ethnicity, or some other axis of difference."[15] In this respect, the AIDS memorial quilt, an ongoing project seeking to name the victims of AIDS worldwide which started in 1985, is a historically important marker of a counter-public. This is a subject which has been explored at length in Marita Sturken's Tangled Memories.[16] This quilt not only created a new type of public memorial form, mobile and participatory in terms of creative production, it also made a moral claim to broaden inclusivity of love and lives that matter in America and elsewhere. In doing so, it sought to shape and broaden larger transnational publics of feeling and consciousness. This memorial is replicated in SL and its presence a testament to the goal orientations of SL LGBTIQ communities and networks. At the same time, as Dunn's research shows, intersections of gender and race (and disability) mediate "queer counterpublics" to reveal hierarchies of commemorative value where white,

[13] Chei Sian Lee and Dion Hoe-Lian Goh, "'Gone Too Soon': Did Twitter Grieve for Michael Jackson?," *Online Information Review* 37, no. 3 (June 14, 2013): 462–78, https://doi.org/10.1108/OIR-05-2012-0082; Jimmy Sanderson and Pauline Hope Cheong, "Tweeting Prayers and Communicating Grief Over Michael Jackson Online," *Bulletin of Science, Technology & Society* 30, no. 5 (October 1, 2010): 328–40, https://doi.org/10.1177/0270467610380010.

[14] L Berlant, *The Female Complaint. The Unfinished Business of Sentimentality in American Culture* (Durham and London: Duke University Press, 2008); M Warner, *Publics and Counter-Publics* (New York: Zone Books, 2002).

[15] R Asen and D Brouwer, *Counterpublics and the State* (Albany: State University of New York Press, 2001), 7.

[16] Tangled Memories: The Vietnam War, the AIDS Epidemic, and the Politics of Remembering (Berkeley: University of California Press, 1997).

cisgender gay men have more visibility and greater backing of financial resources to fund commemorative historical sites of gay liberation and symbols of political activism.[17] For Dunn the AIDS memorial quilt is an important marker of queer intervention into commemorative forms, values, and subjects, but it is also part of a larger gender hierarchy of male privilege in public commemorative culture.[18]

The virtual creation of memorials that acknowledge, mark, and bring to affective community events of violence and tragedy in real life is always dependent on the persistence of virtual communities overtime that have social agendas. Second Life is a social geography in which social agendas for change and recognition are exercised through commemorative places and groups.

The transformative capacity of the internet is that it circumvents the regulatory capacity of nations and governments to determine who or what will be part of public commemorative culture. The absence of commemorative practice in actual physical space—the gravitas of significance and memory conservation through rootedness in physical space—is what the internet transcends. In other words, commemorative hegemonies controlled and exercised by governmental authorities are circumvented in digital commemorative culture.

The commemorative culture in SL materialises the grievability of second lives as semi-autonomous as well as the grievability of more blended lives and, indeed, the grievability of lives lived outside the virtual environment. In the remainder of this chapter, we explore more specifically the culture around commemorating and remembering important people and events. We describe the phenomenon of SL cemeteries in which people and animals, both existing within and outside of the virtual world, are memorialised. We also consider public memorials such as the memorial created as a space to observe the international Transgender Day of Remembrance. While there is very little research on the memorial culture of SL, some important work has been done in this space concerning the Holocaust Memorial Kristallnacht and vernacular memorials in SL and in game worlds more generally.[19]

[17] Thomas Dunn, "Whence the Lesbian in Queer Monumentality? Intersections of Gender and Sexuality in Public Memory," *Southern Communication Journal* 82, no. 4 (2017): 203–15.

[18] Dunn.

[19] Anna Haverinen, "Memoria Virtualis—Death and Mourning Rituals in Online Environments" (University of Turku, 2014), http://www.doria.fi/handle/10024/98454; Bryoni Trezise, "Touching Virtual Trauma: Performative Empathics in Second Life," *Memory Studies* 5, no. 4 (October 1, 2012): 392–409, https://doi.org/10.1177/1750698011426355.

SL also has a tier of memorial culture that does not necessarily coalesce around a spatial memorial but rather groups dedicated to remembering particular events of violence, war, and natural disasters. These include groups which seek to remember the Vietnam War, the Virginia Tech shootings in the USA, the 1986 Chernobyl disaster, and Romanian victims of the Holocaust, to name only a few examples. There are also hundreds of remembrance groups to deceased SL residents, some with dedicated memorials on private individual or group land. There are also many fan groups dedicated to deceased musicians and celebrities such as Elvis Presley, Michael Jackson, Amy Winehouse, Prince, Steve Irwin, and Steve Jobs. These fan groups exist alongside groups dedicated to celebrities who remain alive.

The existence of memorial groups highlights the fact that more immediately recognisable forms of memorialisation such as purchasing space in cemeteries or constructing dedicated memorial parks or buildings require financial capital. While the investment required is far less than would be necessary to construct a memorial offline, it can still be prohibitive to some residents. Groups provide a cheaper alternative.

The types of people and events memorialised in groups are diverse, but they still fall within what might be understood as the broader politics of grieving within SL. This politics unsurprisingly extends and produces (not simply reproduces) hierarchies of grief within a global and often nationalist context. This becomes an important recognition of the kind of potential neocolonialism and imperialism of US-centric emotionalism around the grievability and value of American lives as they become situated within avatar and virtual-world cultures. The memorial culture of SL highlights limitations as to who or what is grievable through monuments, memorial sites, special days of remembrance, and cemeteries. One of the most extensive commemorative histories in SL is September 11, 2001. It spawned the September 11 Avatar Creation Project group who are "concerned with the proliferation of the 9/11 awareness." This is an ambiguous phrase. In a context in which very few people could fail to be aware of the events of 9/11, it leaves itself open to a counter-reading whereby the proliferation of such awareness is a reason to be concerned. By creating an avatar on this date for use in SL only on this date, an awareness of this commemorative date will be practiced through avatar embodiment. This avatar creation is then a birth rite with an inborn sacred status existing for this purpose only and "rezzing"[20] back into life each year only on this commemorative birthdate. This is an

[20] "Rezzing" means making an object or avatar appear.

example of the avatar as memorial, a genre of memorialisation identified and explored in other stories in this book.

Some commemorative spaces in SL are more living than others in terms of signs of continuing visitation such as new and changing objects placed on cemetery plots (such as residents placing gifts at Christmas time). In years of surveying the Second Afterlife Cemetery, we have noticed incremental processes of continuity and change as new plots appear and existing ones disappear. These changes happen with no prefiguring—suddenly a grave is gone, or another arrives next to an existing empty plot, and the social geography has transformed. This is true of all cemeteries to some extent although they are perhaps less spatially and temporally dynamic in terms of change compared to those within virtual social worlds.

We have been struck by the changeability of the memorial culture of SL as a whole. Table 4.1 lists memorials we have encountered during our period of research in SL. These are labelled according to their current status: those still existent at the time of writing are labelled "open," those which have disappeared are labelled "gone," and those whose status remains unclear are labelled "unknown." This list provides an incomplete picture of the range and depth of the memorial culture within SL. One of the most significant memorials in terms of range and depth of relationships and circumstances of death and mourning was the *Remember Our Friends Memorial.* It closed on March 1, 2013, and advertised in advance a series of commemorative events to ritually enact and formalise its closure. These commemorative events allowed residents to, in essence, memorialise the memorial—to return to a place in which they had grieved their lost loved ones and prepare to move the symbolic markers of their grief elsewhere.

Many of these memorials reveal and produce a politics of representation about what histories, nations, and forms of loss, suffering, and bereavement matter by their very materialisation. As a political economy of value, they map and remediate relations of power in a global order. The dominance of memorialisation to citizens of the USA and its constitutive production of nationalism and militarisation in SL memorial culture are pervasive. What is particularly evident in these memorials is the construction of a homogenous audience/viewer—an insider who uncritically aligns with the tone and content of highly masculinist, militarised, nationalist memorial culture. Overwhelmingly, the avatars listed as responsible for military memorials have masculine names and appearances. Conversely, there is commemorative scarcity in relation to national war memorial agendas from other nation-states within SL. Most notably, within the American war memorial contexts, there is a complete absence

Table 4.1 List of memorials we encountered in SL

Public memorials	*Status*
Arianne's Gallery Garden, TokyoMainLand	Open
Breast Cancer Tribute Garden	Gone
Cancer Victims and Survivors Memorial	Gone
Carthage Memorial	Open
Chapel of Lights Memorial	Open
The Church of the Mac	Open
David Bowie Memorial	Open
Day of Remembrance Memorial Garden	Open
Dreams and Dream Traveller	Open
FairChang Memorial Park	Open
Fallen Soldiers Memorial	Open
Garden of Absentia	Open
LGBT History and Memorial Center	Open
Iraqi War Memorial	Open
Holocaust Memorial Museum	Open
Linden Memorial Park Candle Beach	Open
Living Memories Memorial Garden	Open
Memorial for the Fallen	Open
Memorial of the Lost	Open
Memorial Temple of Friends and Loves	Open
Memorial to the Victims of Communism	Gone
Memorial to Victims of Terrorism Throughout the World	Open
Memoriam of Loved Ones	Open
Monumento Malvinas Argentinas	Open
911 Memorial	Open
Operation Enduring Freedom Memorial	Open
Peace Valley Pet Cemetery	Open
Remembering Our Friends Memorial (a ceremonial event was held to close the memorial in 2013)	Gone
Second Afterlife Cemetery	Open
Tailspinners Rest Memorial	Open
The Arch of Valor	Open
The Path to Freedom (memorial to Honour U.S.A. Armed Forces)	Open
The Permanent Pulse Orlando Memorial	Open
Whispers Grave Corporation (WGC) Memorial Gardens	Unknown
Willum Tosung Funeral Home, Cemetery and Memorial Park	Open

of any recognition of civilian deaths within the war geographies and histories that they map such as those of Vietnam, Iraq, and Afghanistan. However, there are memorial sims and groups that are counter-publics of remembrance and memorialisation. Again, LGBTQI groups are particularly active in SL commemorative practices with a range of events including fundraising to support victims of hate crimes.

There is a protective aspect to some of the commemorative groups in SL who may be more vulnerable to harassment than others. While most groups allow easy membership—just a matter pressing the word "join"—this action is just one step in a larger process of becoming a known and trusted member of a group. Once trust is established, a member could then be given the teleport address to a memorial located on a private- or group-owned sim. Trolling on memorials does happen in SL, but it can be transitory rather than persistent. However, many memorials are designed to disable the capacity to trash a site, remove objects, or bring offensive material into a memorial sim.

The Memorial to Victims of Terrorism is a counter-public in which diverse events/circumstances of violence and death are located in a single sim under the name of Terrorism. The sim includes some of the following dedicated memorial text:

> Pray for Baghdad—the Worst Hit of All!;
> Pray for Syria;
> Pray for People of Syria;
> Pray for Istanbul; Pray for St Petersburg;
> Pray for Manhattan;
> Pray for Mogadishu;
> Pray for Las Vegas!;
> Pray for Manchester;
> Pray for London;
> Pray for the Sufi's [SP] of Pakistan!;
> Pray for Kabul;
> Pray for Barcelona and Cambrils;
> Never Forget 9/11!; and
> Pray for the Coptic Christians in Egypt.

Each of these prayer names has a donation option attached to it so that a donor can effectively choose an allegiance and keep this particular prayer commemoration active or alive into the future. By designing for the possibility of individualised commemorative allegiance that is individually monetised, competition and a possible hierarchy of grievability are set up by default. The memorial invokes the action of prayer in the phrase "pray for …." This religious coding is associated with a sense of reverence and solemnity. In *Religion in Secular Society*, noted sociologist Bryan Wilson indicated that non-religious people may nonetheless turn to the church to provide a sense of solemnity at events such as funerals or weddings.[21] The injunction to "pray," despite its explicitly religious meaning, also serves as a suggestion to donate and a reminder to take the losses highlighted seriously. It does not necessarily suggest that action or remembrance ought to be undertaken only by people of faith. However, it is a more passive, individualised response to commemoration and not a communal politics calling for action in protest or dissent.

This is a memorial which is situated within a broadly US-centric commemorative culture wherein the victims of terrorism are more grievable than the victims of US military action. It is a public memorial directed towards the SL community at large. However, this type of broad public facing memorial is far from the most common type in SL. One of the challenges facing any sociologist who seeks to map the memorial culture of SL is the proliferation of memorial cultures which fit under that umbrella. Indeed, particularly robust communities centred on an identity and/or language group in SL are reasonably likely to have their own memorial culture. For example, the Romanian community in SL has many different types of sims linked to places and cultural histories and includes its own Holocaust memorial. Given the centrism of USA as a political and social geography in SL, we have been surprised by the limited number of memorials specifically dedicated to mass shooting events such as Sutherland Springs church (2017), Mandalay Bay, Las Vegas (2017), Sandy Hook (2012), and Aurora, Colorado shootings (2012) and the absence of discussion of these events in community forums. The politics of commemoration is revealed in absence as much as presence. It is possible that these events are not commemorated because they are not specifically linked to particular identity groups or personal losses within SL in the way that other memorials clearly are. However, memorials dedicated to these particular events would probably mean that the creator is actively taking up the issue of gun control, and this might well be a subject yet to find its commemorative voice in SL.

In an early period of our research, MargieG interviewed the owner of the memorial to the victims of communism. This memorial no longer exists. The owner, a citizen of the USA, created this memorial because it represented her own family history of suffering and persecution (including in gulags) under communism in the former Soviet Union. The memorial

[21] Bryan R. Wilson, *Religion in Secular Society: A Sociological Comment* (Watts, 1966).

had a postbox inviting people to tell their stories of suffering under communist regimes. This memorial experienced a number of trolling incidents and became embroiled in territorial conflict with a sim dedicated to a positive representation of communism and socialist philosophy, deliberately set up on land right next door. This trolling may have stemmed mainly from bullying directed at this person than from actual opposition to the memorial itself. We have found evidence to suggest that this person has been the victim of extensive trolling both within and outside of SL. Setting aside for a moment the fact that the memorial to communism came out of a distinct personal and family history, its very presence also speaks to the absence of a memorial counterpart. Capitalism has its own past and present victims—lives diminished and cut short through dangerous working conditions, processes of exploitation, and the economic drivers of war. However, it is not possible to mourn, as a whole, the victims of a political economy that cannot be imagined as situated in the historical past as dead and gone. In the Western social imaginary of the cold war battle, capitalism won over communism; the capitalist and democratic West defeated the political economy of the communist East. Capitalism has not become an object of world history as something that has passed into non-being. It exists (it is not dead) and therefore its victims cannot be mourned as a whole, as though they existed in a historical past. At the same time, imagining the end of capitalism, a persistent theme in Marxist thought places this economic system on a trajectory in which it could enter into future commemorative history.

The memorial culture of SL of course itself exists within the context of the internet, which itself is Americanised, as evidenced by the preponderance of English-language content and the very organisation of web addresses, with the websites of American companies, governments, and organisations ending in a suffix which denotes their function (.gov; .edu; .org) and those in other countries ending in a country identifier (.au for Australia, .ca for Canada, etc.).[22] As such the internet has been described as a tool of "deep imperialism" which often goes unnoticed and unchallenged.[23] This type of unnoticed imperialism is evident in SL. While there is no official language, the vast majority of residents speak in English. Where they cannot or prefer not to use English, residents will often use a translating device. Margaret has conducted several interviews with residents

[22] Juli L. Gittinger, "Is There Such a Thing as 'cyberimperialism?,'" *Continuum* 28, no. 4 (July 4, 2014): 514, https://doi.org/10.1080/10304312.2014.907873.

[23] Gittinger, "Is There Such a Thing as 'cyberimperialism'?".

who have used such a device. Even places which are specifically designed to replicate cities or other spaces in which the dominant language is not English nonetheless cater for English-speaking residents in their signage. The memorial culture of SL reflects this often invisible American imperialism through the presence of particular kinds of memorials and the absence of others. Even the most personal aspects of this culture such as cemeteries and individual memorials reflect the norms of the Anglosphere.

Cemeteries

SL cemeteries mirror those in the Western nations of the physical world. The most prominent features expansive green lawns, trees, and neatly arranged rows of plots. Headstones are generally grey with a stone-like texture and feature inscriptions with the name of the loved one who has died. A high proportion of gravesites feature images. These images may be integrated into the headstone but may also take the form of framed photographs placed elsewhere on the gravesite. In some cases, the headstone acts as a screen on which a story is told through a series of images. In a previous publication, Margaret wrote about a young woman with many SL families who was killed by her RL partner. Members of all of her SL families came together to create a memorial.[24] Her headstone features a series of family photographs. The young woman is shown in RL, with her baby. She is shown with members of her SL families. The headstone provides a sense of a life lived both online and offline and a person who was well loved in both worlds. The very act of coming together to create such a memorial may be understood as an act of "elective affinity" on the part of the young woman's SL families.

The form these cemeteries take is rooted in hidden cultural meaning. While lawn cemeteries as quiet spaces of reflection and remembrance are a form familiar to many residents, one does not need to look too far afield to find variations of this in the physical world. The cemeteries of New Orleans, for example, serve as spaces not just of memory but also of recovery and community connection.[25] The cemeteries of Mexico City invite

[24] Margaret Gibson, "Grievable Lives: Avatars, Memorials, and Family 'Plots' in Second Life," *Mortality* 22 (January 12, 2017): 232, https://doi.org/10.1080/13576275.2016.1263941.

[25] DeMond Shondell Miller and Jason David Rivera, "Hallowed Ground, Place, and Culture: The Cemetery and the Creation of Place," *Space and Culture* 9, no. 4 (November 2006): 334–50, https://doi.org/10.1177/1206331206292450.

and provide for active and ongoing social engagement with the dead.[26] The lawn cemeteries of SL borrow from an aesthetic developed in the twentieth century and popular in the UK, the USA, and other culturally similar nations such as Australia.[27] The dominance of this cemetery form is suggestive of a broadly accepted "correct" way to grieve which is in keeping with contemporary preferences in Western nations. While we have spent a great deal of time in the cemeteries of SL, we have rarely encountered more than one or two residents present at any time. The spaces are also designed to be prohibitive of loud or indiscreet communication with the voice function often disabled. Occasionally, one will witness visitors at cemeteries standing or sitting near plots, but a social code of privacy prevails as one might expect.

In our conversations with residents who own cemeteries or have memorialised loved ones, we have found a range of reasons for participating in this practice. For some residents the purpose is simply to have a place to grieve. These residents are unable to visit the physical gravesite of a person they have lost. This may be because of geographical distance, but it could also be the result of interpersonal issues. One resident to whom we spoke created a SL grave for a man who had been her lover for a decade. She had known him both offline and in SL but had felt that she could not attend his funeral or visit his grave out of respect for his wife, who did not know about the affair. Some communities create cemeteries specifically for their own members. For example, 1920s Berlin, discussed in the chapter on nostalgia, has its own cemetery. It also hosts its own funerals. This is very much a space in which the community which "owned" the resident can mourn.

These are forms of memorialisation which seek to address the loss of a person who has died—or is believed to have died—offline. However, there are also cemeteries in which people are able to bury their own former avatars. As a result, some cemeteries feature a mix of people who have died offline and those who have only died in SL and may in fact return. Who is grievable in terms of being memorialised in this commemorative culture depends on the specific cemetery or space of memory in which grieving occurs.

[26] Marcel Reyes-Cortez, "Material Culture, Magic and the Santa Muerte in the Cemeteries of a Megalopolis," *Culture and Religion* 13, no. 1 (March 2012): 107–31, https://doi.org/10.1080/14755610.2012.658420.

[27] Julie Rugg, "Lawn Cemeteries: The Emergence of a New Landscape of Death," *Urban History* 33, no. 2 (August 2006): 213–33, https://doi.org/10.1017/S0963926806003786.

Butler writes that "[u]ngrievable lives are those that cannot be lost, and cannot be destroyed, because they already inhabit a lost and destroyed zone; they are, ontologically, and from the start, already lost and destroyed, which means that when they are destroyed [...] nothing is destroyed."[28] In a sense, it is possible to view acts of memorialisation which seek to recognise the grievability of lives lived in SL as a form of political action which asserts the reality of such lives. The recognition of the high rate of suicide for people in LGBTQI identities and the global issue of homophobic violence and murder directed at nonnormative sex and gender identities is a politics and protest of grievability claimed within the spatial geography, queer communities, and rituals of SL memorial culture. This is an important counter-public of commemorative culture enabled through a strong community network. At the same time, hearing stories of residents who died as a result of domestic violence speaks to a larger absence of public memorial culture that geographically and symbolically acknowledges a globally massive statistic of largely men's crimes against women who could be memorialised as a group. What would such an act or possible culture of memorialisation say or do? Butler states that "[w]ithout grievability, there is no life, or, rather, there is something living that is other than life."[29] As highlighted in the previous chapter, avatar lives are understood by many residents to be real lives with their own intrinsic value. The corollary of the assertion that these lives are real is that they are grievable and indeed often must be grieved.

Cemeteries in SL primarily operate as a space in which to memorialise two groups of people—those who lived in SL and those who did not but who were important to SL residents. Tony Walter has demonstrated that, in a world in which home and work are separated, grief is shaped by the geographies in which individuals live and the necessity to operate in spheres in which those who never knew the deceased surround one.[30] Such separations are neither necessarily positive nor necessarily negative—they are simply a fact of contemporary life and grief. These divisions are exacerbated in the case of SL, where people who lose significant others known only in-world may find themselves spending most of their time,

[28] Judith Butler, *Frames of War: When Is Life Grievable?*, Pbk. ed. (London ; New York: Verso, 2010), xix.

[29] Butler, 15.

[30] "Grief and the Separation of Home and Work," *Death Studies* 33, no. 5 (May 2009): 402–10, https://doi.org/10.1080/07481180902805616.

both at home and at work, with a community which not only did not know the person who has been lost but who are also not necessarily able to comprehend the loss that has in fact occurred. The digital flesh of SL residents cannot operate unless it is encountered by those who are sympathetic to the moral status of people known only online. For many people who are not themselves SL residents and who have not experienced significant relationships through other digital media, there is no capacity to understand the grievability of an avatar life. As such, the grief and loss experienced by residents may not be met with support from their offline friends, families, or colleagues. When they disconnect from SL, grievers are deprived of the communities of shared grieving wherein their loss can be acknowledged.

The Spirit of Lena Anthony[31] runs the Second Afterlife Cemetery. She is no longer "alive" in SL but maintains an account in order to look after the cemetery. Her avatar takes the form of a ghost. She has her own grave on the cemetery grounds, featuring a date at which she "derezzed" but "refused to cross over." Lena Anthony was the user's first avatar but has now been replaced with an alt. Lena is able to tell stories about many of the people memorialised in her cemetery, some she knew personally and others she has learned about only through the stories of the residents who choose to remember them. Lena's narrative reveals the extensive emotional labour required in her role. One experience which particularly impacted her was meeting a distraught father whose daughter had recently been murdered. She did not use SL herself; however, her father was a regular user. The young woman had been murdered by her partner. "I cried listening to her father's story. He was distraught and just wanted to do something," Lena said.

The Second Afterlife Cemetery initially sold gravesites in perpetuity. Now it offers them for a monthly fee. The impact of this change is that, while some graves remain in the cemetery more or less permanently, others are present only temporarily. In addition, some sites are rented but remain empty. The result is a more transient cemetery space than would exist in the physical world. Gravesites are connected not only to the physical space but also to the ongoing presence of a resident willing to pay maintenance fees. Thus the marker of a significant person's life is removed if the person tasked with maintaining it himself dies or leaves SL. There is no possibility of a permanent or semi-permanent memorial in this space

[31] Real avatar name used.

which is not reliant upon the continued presence of another resident. The gravestones in the Second Afterlife Cemetery, while they retain the appearance of stone associated with physical cemeteries, do not possess the longevity associated with that material. They are in a sense robbed of their discursive association with permanence.

Jane, who was introduced in the previous chapter, is part of a close-knit group of friends formed when they all worked as volunteers assisting new residents. Over time they have lost several members, all of whom are buried in a row of individual plots so that they are together in something akin to a family plot. No members of the group were family "except through friendship." The proximity of the burials, and the fact that they were arranged by members of the group, speaks to the importance of the ties formed within SL. These ties of digital kinship and close friendship networks remain recognisable even after the separation of residents by death. This plot contains a gap where another gravestone once stood. This belonged to a person who was believed to have died but who was found alive. Such cases—where a person believed to be dead is in fact alive and later reappears—are far more common in SL than in the physical world. The ever-present possibility that the dead or missing may reappear problematizes the commemoration and memorialisation of deceased friends and loved ones where emotion can be experienced as wasted and exploited.

Jane and her friends initially constructed memorials at the island where they had worked as volunteers. However, they did not own the island, and after the first few memorials were in place, they were told that no more would be permitted. Four years ago they decided to memorialise their friends at the Second Afterlife Cemetery. There is infighting over how the memorials are maintained. As a result, an avatar has been created which pays for their maintenance and does other necessary tasks. No one in the group (except the person using this avatar) knows who performs this role. This is a means through which infighting is, if not prevented, at least reduced. The necessity of such measures suggests that there is considerable tension over who has the right to be the keeper of memories and, indeed, to determine how memories are kept.

This was not the only instance we encountered of friendships being maintained in death through the strategic allocation of virtual burial plots. Michael, whose relationship with Sarah has been described earlier in this book, has a plot in a small cemetery in a roleplaying sim he frequented. Two weeks before we spoke to Sarah, a friend of his, Cyber, died. They had played opposing roles in the roleplay sim, with Michael playing a pirate and Cyber playing a naval officer. Sarah and her friend ensured that their graves were next to one another so that Michael and Cyber "could play pirates and navy together." Michael was a member of many other roleplaying communities and has small memorials in at least three other sims. The private cemeteries of individual communities are more difficult to find than places like the Second Afterlife Cemetery. Memorials or gravestones in community cemeteries have the capacity to be more permanent. They are rarely rented and instead become part of community landscapes.

One long-lasting grave in the Second Afterlife Cemetery is that of Cole, an academic chemist. He had worked in SL prior to his death, trying to develop open access resources for teaching chemistry. His grave was created by Ellie who was a long-time friend. Ellie describes Cole as a brilliant man, a person who was driven by his conscience and a real desire to share knowledge and create social change. He had been depressed for many years. Ellie and Cole were close in both RL and SL, and when she learned he had committed suicide, her first responses were not just shock and sadness but also anger. She said,

> He knew he could come to me when he was in a bad place. Not for sex or anything like that. But just to sit still and be with someone who could sit still next to him. He didn't reach out. He had reached out so many times over ten years. I talk him out of the tree so many times before. But this time he didn't reach out and I am mad at him for that.

She made a grave for him and held a small ceremony on her own in SL. Ellie was very aware that their friendship, close as it was, would not be recognised by Cole's other friends and family. Only in SL did she feel able to grieve the loss of this significant relationship. Cole's headstone features an image of his avatar. Ellie does not visit very often, choosing to pay the rental fee a year at a time. Every time she visits she finds that the graves near Cole's have changed.

There is a disconnect between the practices of mourning employed in the Second Afterlife Cemetery and the responses of some residents who do not share the same definition of the situation as the grievers. Trolls—people who engage in a form of play directed at causing distress and discomfort in other residents—have targeted the cemetery on a few occasions. According to The Spirit of Lena Anthony:

> Once I arrived and was immediately swarmed by zombies. Then they followed me no matter where I went. LOL I actually thought it was kind of funny though not at all appropriate for here.

Another incident, which she did not find amusing, involved a person spawning flying pornographic images in the cemetery. While Linden Labs has largely eliminated the exploits which allow people to wreak havoc in this way, there are other, subtler, ways to troll serious locations such as appearing in a sim naked.

Despite the many differences between SL cemeteries and those offline—particularly the changeability of gravesites and the presence of trolls—residents who have memorialised loved ones emphasise the similarities. Desiderus had a year-long relationship with a partner he had met only in SL. He did not meet her in RL or exchange pictures, nor did he wish to do so.

> We really did not to have SL cross over into RL to that degree. There are many kinds of interests in what people want in SL but it often baffles me that people believe that this is a 'second' life and don't want to meet other people in RL but still exchange pictures. We create our own images in here.

Towards the end of their relationship, however, the ill health which impacted her physical body became a key factor in their relationship. Desiderus became worried about her health. When she died he experienced grief—a grief he felt the need to justify. He emphasised that even though the relationship was entirely in SL, "emotions such as the sadness of her loss is real to me in RL." Desiderus indicated that his grief was real because he felt it outside of SL—that is, it was felt by the typist who controlled the avatar rather than being attributable to or enacted by the avatar itself.

Desiderus created a memorial to his SL partner and we asked how he used it. He said:

> I think it's pretty much like how people are in RL. I used to go almost every day. Now it's more like every so often. Every week or two I go and sit. When I go I remember our wonderful times. I have to admit … not all relationships in SL are so free of drama. But she and I had a magnificent year.

This need to memorialise the loss of a partner known only in SL was shared by other residents we interviewed. Clark created a gravesite for his SL partner, Linda. They had been together in SL for seven months prior to her death. They had not met in RL but had intended to do so. He described Linda:

> Linda was very healthy before [her illness]. She jogged, worked out at a gym every day and was in very good shape. Her illness was very sudden. She was

> a very kind person, she would cook dinner for the elderly neighbour next door, she was funny and we loved making each other love. She was very active in her community and loved having her daughter and Grandson visit. She was at the time going through a bitter divorce and liked the fact that I was a good listener.

Unlike Desiderus, Clark had lost a relationship which he fully intended to transfer into physical reality. His loss was then not only the loss of a companion and lover in SL—which is significant in and of itself—but also the loss of an imagined future in which he and Linda would have enjoyed a physical romantic relationship. Clark's current SL partner encouraged him to set up his memorial for Linda. Unlike most gravestones in SL, Linda's does not contain an image of her avatar. Instead, it features a smiling older woman. He said "all avatars have another one of them [meaning that avatars are not truly unique]. For me Linda was one of a kind, someone seeing this memorial will know what we had was in real life too." Both Clark and Desiderus emphasised the reality of their feelings of grief and loss in the face of the death of a loved one they had met only within SL. They did so through presenting their loss as a real loss which they felt in their embodied lives. Their emphasis on the reality of their loss suggests that they did not see their grief as self-explanatory due to the connection of their relationships to SL.

Others used SL as a space in which to memorialise relationships which were recognisable and grievable offline but which demanded recognition beyond that which could occur elsewhere. Aida created a headstone for her RL brother in SL. He was not a resident of SL; however, Aida said:

> I made a memorial for him because it made me feel close. To see his pic on a daily basis keeps me and my heart sane. It was a huge loss for me. The last time I heard his actual voice was almost five years ago, two years before he passed.

Aida's brother's real body had been cremated and entombed. There was no photograph at his marker. This is, for Aida, insufficient. The impersonal tomb fails to provide her with a sense of closeness and connection to her sibling. Aida needed a more personal space of memory, one which she could visit at her leisure and at which she could view her brother's face and remember. His photograph is featured on his headstone. She visits the gravesite three times a week to reflect upon her life and talk to her brother.

While her RL sister has also died, it occurred in the mid-1990s. She said she never considered creating a memorial to her sister in SL. The fact that her brother passed away after memorialisation in SL became a possibility for her was an important factor in her decision-making. Aida had already come to terms with the death of her sister and the conditions under which mourning this loss was possible. It was only in the face of a fresh loss that she saw SL as a necessary and appropriate space in which to enact her grief.

Not every resident believes that SL cemeteries and funerals are beneficial. In 2011 MargieG created a forum post asking SL residents if they would like a funeral in SL if they died. Responses were mixed. Some respondents indicated that they believed people did not die in SL. "Coffins are for vampire [roleplay]," one response read. Others explained how SL cemeteries work. One resident indicated that the question was insensitive as it could be read by someone who was dying. Another resident indicated that in SL people could "die" and reappear—in that an avatar may become inactive, and their friends could believe they had died. The very reality of death in SL is contested alongside the actual grievability of avatar lives.

Another resident said they would like a respectful notice sent to their friends, not a funeral. They indicated that their friends only knew a fictional character, not "them." "If someone in SL has formed a close enough attachment to the real person behind the avatar, such that their passing would merit attending a funeral, then I think attending the real life funeral, or holding a private observance in the real world, would be far more meaningful than doing any ceremony in a virtual world."

Public Memorials

Extensive research has explored the way in which the internet has been used for public acts of grieving.[32] Online memorials offer a democratised space in which grief can be expressed immediately and by a wide range of people who may otherwise not have a right to speak. Such grief has commemorated the loss of important social and cultural figures but also major

[32] Sian Lee and Hoe-Lian Goh, "'Gone Too Soon'"; Nataliya Danilova, "The Politics of Mourning: The Virtual Memorialisation of British Fatalities in Iraq and Afghanistan," *Memory Studies* 8, no. 3 (July 2015): 267–81, https://doi.org/10.1177/1750698014563874; R. N. McEwen and K. Scheaffer, "Virtual Mourning and Memory Construction on Facebook: Here Are the Terms of Use," *Bulletin of Science, Technology & Society* 33, no. 3–4 (June 1, 2013): 64–75, https://doi.org/10.1177/0270467613516753; Carroll and Landry, "Logging On and Letting Out"; Gibson, "Grievable Lives."

events in public memory. For example, September 11 was memorialised in a range of ways online immediately after the events.[33] The physical memorial to these events plays an important role in determining the dominant mode of retrospectively understanding and recovering. This memorial is a place of memory imbued with the rhetoric of resilience.[34] The continued impact of physical memorials, despite the fact that they take far longer to construct than the online form, indicates that a sense of place is a key factor in remembrance. SL, unlike an ordinary website, allows users to create a place in which they, in a physical form, can go and remember.

At the time of our research, we found three memorials to 9/11 (Fig. 4.1). On September 11, 2016, US time, Clara Coates spent a few hours in each of these memorials. Even the largest memorial only seemed to be populated by one other person at a time. People teleported in, stayed for a few moments, and then were gone. There were no mass rituals of memory. This behaviour seems to suggest a desire for a ritual—or interest in one if it exists—but no impetus to do the work of creating this sort of ritual of remembering. However, despite the apparent lack of interest, the memorials remain. Not surprisingly, perhaps, the heroic narrative of American imperialism as identified in a great of research post-9/11 remembrance and commemoration is embedded and repeated in SL. This includes the rhetoric not just of resilience, as stated earlier, but a code of heroic invulnerability. One of the memorials is a room dominated by a window through which the Twin Towers remain visible and unchanged. This recuperative act re-covers the symbolic wound of their destruction, asserting the idea of America's indestructability as a national community and ideal. This schism in the memorial creates a tension between the avowal and disavowal of loss and change.

These are part of a memorial culture that is highly militarised and US-centric. Lloyd refers to an order of grievability, described as "the hierarchical organisation of who counts as a fully human subject and thus whose lives matter."[35] She notes that the deaths of specific populations, such as

[33] Aaron Hess, "In Digital Remembrance: Vernacular Memory and the Rhetorical Construction of Web Memorials," *Media, Culture & Society* 29, no. 5 (September 2007): 812–30, https://doi.org/10.1177/0163443707080539.

[34] Nicholas S. Paliewicz, "Bent But Not Broken: Remembering Vulnerability and Resiliency at the National September 11 Memorial Museum," *Southern Communication Journal* 82, no. 1 (January 2017): 11, https://doi.org/10.1080/1041794X.2016.1252422.

[35] Moya Lloyd, "Naming the Dead and the Politics of the 'human,'" *Review of International Studies* 43, no. 2 (April 2017): 268, https://doi.org/10.1017/S0260210516000358.

Fig. 4.1 MargieG visiting a memorial to the events of September 11, 2001

Palestinian populations, may not be ungrievable per se but instead ungrievable within the order perpetuated by mainstream Western media.[36] In this context their deaths are reported and considered arithmetically rather than through the names and faces accorded to the grievable. It is precisely this according of faces and names that features in the military-style memorials we explored in SL. The politics of grievability and ungrievability operate in SL much as they do in the physical landscapes of Western nations.

Memorials to military engagement play an important role in developing and perpetuating the militarised culture of the USA. Such memorials, despite the fact that they serve as spaces of memory for those lost in the often distant past, are in fact deeply rooted in the needs of the present. The National World War II memorial in Washington, for instance, has been described as promoting gratitude and reciprocity as a basis for membership in the national community.[37] Their presence in SL indicates a

[36] Lloyd, 270.

[37] Erika Doss, "War, Memory, and the Public Mediation of Affect: The National World War II Memorial and American Imperialism," *Memory Studies* 1, no. 2 (May 2008): 246–47, https://doi.org/10.1177/1750698007088388.

similar expectation of gratitude and reciprocation which is comprehensible only through an understanding of the unspoken and unquestioned dominance of US culture in this presumably multinational environment.

In the context of a militarised US-centric environment, it is perhaps unsurprising that there is an absence of memorialisation of the victims of US military action. As Gregory notes of the war in Afghanistan:

> By reducing Afghans to absolute victims, the dominant representations of the war in Afghanistan foreclosed the possibility that they could be recognised as anything more than potential humans, humans-yet-to-be. The deaths of Afghans cannot, therefore, be mourned because they are already seen as lost, their humanity forever deferred.[38]

This is in keeping with Butler's analysis. She states that war depends on a distribution of grievability in which some lives are necessarily ungrievable.[39] The focus on US events and military memorials is evident in the list provided on the SL Destination Guide. At the time of writing, 13 memorials are listed on the destination guide.[40] This list does not encompass all of the memorials available in SL. It is, however, indicative of the nature of more popular destinations within SL's commemorative culture. The prevalence of militarised and US-focused memorials does not indicate, however, that these are especially popular or receive high levels of traffic. Indeed, we have visited these sites at various times of the day and year and have never found more than two other residents present. These memorials, then, do not serve as centres for mass acts of grief and memory. Instead, they serve to define the lives that are grievable and important within the context of SL. Public memorials in a sense operate primarily for the purpose of being used in rituals associated with specific days and acts of remembrance.

In at least one instance, a memorial created in SL serves to assert the grievability of lives lost offline. Random Demina[41] operates the Transgender

[38] Thomas Gregory, "Potential Lives, Impossible Deaths: AFGHANISTAN, CIVILIAN CASUALTIES AND THE POLITICS OF INTELLIGIBILITY," *International Feminist Journal of Politics* 14, no. 3 (September 2012): 341–42, https://doi.org/10.1080/14616742.2012.659851.

[39] Butler, *Frames of War*, xix.

[40] "Memorials in Second Life," Second Life, accessed August 14, 2017, http://secondlife.com/destinations/memorial.

[41] We use Random Demina's real avatar name here as it is impossible to discuss her work without providing sufficient clues for an informed person to ascertain her identity.

Hate Crime & Suicide Memorial. She has limited financial resources and often struggles to pay the tier, or monthly fee, required for the maintenance of the land. However, the memorial is an important part of her life and her advocacy. Even though she sometimes finds herself unable to maintain the expense, she always comes back to SL and re-establishes the memorial. She explains that

> Transwomen keep getting murdered and assaulted. Social stigmas keep them at a high suicide rate. It's needed and someone has to do it. The desire to have this memorial running became a huge part of who I am, and I brought it back as soon as it was possible. It took six years, while I went through my own hard times.

The memorial features many candles with the names of trans people who have died. It also has large pillars with names on them. A sign reads: "[v]isitors can get in touch with me to request a candle lit, and the names on the pillars come from the Transgender Day of Remembrance database." The Transgender Day of Remembrance, held on November 11, is a key date in the life of the memorial. Each year a small service is held during which Random Demina reads out a list of transgender people who have died through murder or suicide during the year. MargieG attended the 2016 event and found that many of the people who had died were based in Brazil. The accuracy and completeness of the list are uncertain. As a group, transgender people are marginalised everywhere, but particularly in nations with forms of legislation and social policy which are restrictive rather than protective or open. In SL, this group is rendered explicitly and openly mournable in a way which might not be possible elsewhere. The SL space of memorialisation can speak back to deficiencies in both national systems of power and physical-world mourning cultures. The SL ceremony is highly emotive. The presence of a handful of residents serves to assert that these lives are meaningful, grievable, and grieved.

There is power in the act of reading the names of the deceased. Naming the dead is a form of rehumanising the unnamed, of making their lives matter.[42] A similar determination to name those who have been lost is evident in the practice of constructing memorial gardens. Lynette created a memorial garden in order to help her remember friends and loved ones lost in SL and offline. MargieG spoke to her first in 2015 and again in 2017.

[42] Lloyd, "Naming the Dead and the Politics of the 'human,'" 271.

At the second meeting, Lynette revealed that she had added a second level to her garden. Residents are able to have a plaque added to the garden by simply sending her a message. Often residents just want a name on a plaque. However, there are occasions when they ask to have a photograph, either from RL or SL, included. Most do not include their own names on the plaques. "I did not put my name on my parents' one there. I guess like in a real graveyard. You only usually have the deceased on the headstones." The name of the deceased, separated from the person who chose for them to be memorialised, provides them a sense of personhood distinct from the mourner. Unlike in the Second Afterlife Cemetery, there is no rental fee for memorials in Lynette's garden.

Some other memorials are dedicated to the memory of a single important resident. Eagle created a memorial hall for a man who rented land from him for many years. Sal was a man who loved to use SL to participate in fishing and sailing. He was heavily involved in the SL sailing community. Sal disappeared for several months, and Eagle and his friends became concerned. They were relieved to see him log on one day—however, it turned out to be his son. The son had discovered the SL client logged on to his father's computer. He informed them that Sal had died. At the time Eagle was building a dance venue on his land. He asked permission from Sal's son to turn it into a memorial. Permission was granted. An image of Sal's SL avatar is featured in the memorial. Eagle described his decision to memorialise his friend in this way:

> I realised then that those large places with "Memorial" in their names were named in that fashion, so that the memory of our friends and loved ones may live on [...] I know that every time we use the venue I'll salute Sal and drink a virtual toast in his name.

Eagle's decision to create a living memorial—a space of memory which could be used for ordinary events rather than a space specifically and exclusively designed for memory—reflects the forms of memorialisation privileged in the USA in the immediate aftermath of World War II.[43] Such a form of memorialisation brings the memory of the dead into the routines of daily life rather than sequestering such memories within a specific and designated location which serves no other function.

[43] Doss, "War, Memory, and the Public Mediation of Affect," 231.

In SL, the scope of what can be commemorated or mourned, and the means through which this can occur, is relatively open. In the context of physical world political geographies, it is much more difficult to claim physical spaces as sites for public mourning and memory. In SL, residents can create their own spaces for mourning without needing to pass through the state in order to legitimise forms of mourning that have a public orientation and even an educative function around the question of grievable lives. Part of the function of the democratic state is to mediate between competing narratives and forms of storytelling, including mourning. Without this mediating body, residents must personally engage in mediation and contestation around the mournability of particular objects or people. Without the intervention of the state, debates about types of human value and forms of mournability are enacted on the sites of memorials themselves. While the scope of what can be grieved is more open, there is a paradoxical effect wherein the very fact that residents do not need to obtain official governmental forms of permission opens up controversial memorials to forms of trolling or incursions which themselves serve to delegitimise forms of memory. In our engagement with more vulnerable communities there was a protective reticence around access to these more vulnerable memorial spaces and rituals. The residents who operate memorials can become a type of quasi-public figure and can therefore become open to a sense of potential victimisation. They may become both caretakers and gatekeepers in relation to spaces of memory in SL.

CHAPTER 5

Sentimental Objects

Introduction

In 2017 Bandai America released a 20th anniversary edition of the ubiquitous 1990s toy, Tamagotchi.[1] This toy, beloved by a generation, simulates the experience of owning a pet. It is a physical object through which the user can feed, wash, and otherwise care for a black- and-white digital creature. The pet on the Tamagotchi screen hatches, lives, and dies. At every stage of its life cycle, it demands care and attention. In 1999, the website Neopets was launched, allowing children to create their own digital pets. Like Tamagotchi pets, Neopets required daily acts of care and attention. Unlike Tamagotchis, Neopets could not die. Wrye has suggested that such virtual pets challenge notions of pets as inherently and necessarily existing as living creatures. Instead, she argues that pets should be understood in relation to an idea of petness which would encompass such virtual creatures.[2] Sherry Turkle noted that children had, by the turn of the twenty-first century, learned to differentiate between types of

[1] Kaya Yurieff, "Tamagotchi's 20th Anniversary Pet Is as Demanding as Ever," CNNMoney, October 10, 2017, http://money.cnn.com/2017/10/10/technology/tamagotchi-mini/index.html.

[2] Jen Wrye, "Beyond Pets: Exploring Relational Perspectives of Petness," *Canadian Journal of Sociology* 34, no. 4 (2009): 1022–63.

M. Gibson, C. Carden, *Living and Dying in a Virtual World*,
Palgrave Macmillan Memory Studies,
https://doi.org/10.1007/978-3-319-76099-5_5

"alive" and types of "love." Thus they could feel a particular type of love for their digital pet which they perceived as being in a sense alive.[3]

In essence, virtual pets are digital objects which have the potential to become important as sentimental objects with which the user maintains a relationship. This is an unusually coherent example of a more widespread phenomenon: the development of sentimental relationships with digital objects. While virtual pets may be placed aside as their users age, they are replaced with other meaningful objects which may themselves be digital. Thus the connection to digital objects is not only the space of childhood. Our memories of childhood are in a sense screen memories[4] and have been for some time. We remember films and television shows, and, if we are part of a younger cohort, we remember video games and virtual pets. But as we grow and age, we remain connected to screens and to forms of digital connection. We also come to remember our previous digital attachments as meaningful relationships.

When people enter SL, they bring memories of home, childhood, fragments, and spectres of past times, lost places, the living, and the dead. They also bring aspirations and fantasies for community, friendship, sex, love, and belonging. While the previous chapter explores the public aspect of material culture in relation to grievability, this chapter explores the more personalised and domestic objects that are related to memories of lost and deceased friends, lovers, and experiences. The nearly unlimited ability to create objects is one of SL's most appealing and well-publicised features. It is at the heart of what Boellstorff describes as "creationist capitalism."[5] In this chapter we discuss those objects to which SL residents have a sentimental attachment. We discuss the way in which objects can serve as reminders of loved ones who have either died or moved on. We also discuss the way in which SL residents consciously replicate and reproduce meaningful objects they encounter outside of SL such as items relating to home, clothing, and even pets. Finally, we consider the fate of objects whose owners have "died"—either virtually, through ceasing to enter the virtual world, or through the physical death of the person behind the avatar.

[3] Sherry Turkle, "Cuddling up to Cyborg Babies," *UNESCO Courier* 53, no. 9 (2000): 43–45.

[4] Harvey Roy Greenberg, *Screen Memories: Hollywood Cinema on the Psychoanalytic Couch* (New York, NY: Columbia University Press, 1993).

[5] Tom Boellstorff, *Coming of Age in Second Life: An Anthropologist Explores the Virtually Human* (Princeton and Oxford: Princeton University Press, 2008).

Digital objects have been described as "simply objects on the Web,"[6] that is, the vast array of photographs, videos, and websites which we may access through the screens of our computers or mobile phones. These objects are inescapable. However, they are also in a sense removed from our embodied selves. We may scroll past a digital object, interact with it, save it, or in some cases print it and render it physical. In SL, there is an added dimension of felt materiality. The embodied self as avatar is able to pick up, carry, wear, or alter digital objects. In the everydayness of digital lives, this is part of the materiality that grounds our very existence. Furthermore, we cannot internally conjure an image of self or other without locating an embodiment in time and space, including digital spaces. In a digital age, embodiment is often through avatars, which may or may not take a 3D human form. In Turkle's earlier work on screen life and virtual communities, the computer is figured as a porous "Alice through the looking glass" portal where people step into other realities of discovery and sociality.[7] In virtual worlds the computer screen is also equally a barrier and mask for social and emotional distancing between the projected virtual world self or roleplay character and the self behind the screen. While most of our interviewees treat SL as place in which they are not that much different from their RL self or personality, for others it is a place of fictional lives and characters, and the expectation and pursuit of deep emotional connection that is carried into real life are not wanted and rejected.

In SL, the representational body through which participants act and relate to each other is not just simply a projected image but rather a textual body made of conversational histories, gestures, shared experiences, and intimacies of feeling. Over time the avatar accrues through its social history and storied life what we have been calling digital flesh. This embedded, narratively thick life gives moral weight to the representational body in the social and intimate connections people make, develop, and hold. The use of voice in SL also imprints the avatar with the physical person behind the screen both exposing and enmeshing its presence through an auditory, vocal trace. As we have stated earlier, affective states, emotions, and thought processes happen with and through the body behind the

[6] Yuk Hui, "What Is a Digital Object?," *Metaphilosophy* 43, no. 4 (2012): 380.

[7] Sherry Turkle and Simon & Schuster, *Life on the Screen: Identity in the Age of the Internet* (New York, NY [etc.: Simon & Schuster Paperbacks : sold by Amazon Digital Services LLC, 2011).

screen with the avatar as representation and instantiation of this connective flesh.

Physical and digital objects are both important in the perception of self or memories of the other. Their meaning is transformed at or before the moment of loss, and they serve as a reminder and remainder of a person who is irrevocably gone. However, objects can become significant, meaningful, and loved without the added poignancy of association with loss. Objects can form one way of presenting the self and telling a life story.[8] They offer topics for conversation and the means through which significant ideas can be communicated. Nagy and Koles sought to understand the avatar-self relationship and the way in which people become attached to virtual objects. Their study, which involved people constructing avatars, found that virtual objects such as pets were seen as essential in individualising the avatar. Objects served to highlight the characteristics associated with the virtual self.[9] These authors were performing research in an environment in which objects were pre-created and limited. In SL this is not the case. The creationist capitalist ethos of SL has led to a situation in which an almost infinite array of objects can be created or purchased. Thus the possibilities for finding or constructing meaningful objects are expanded significantly. Despite this, we have found that the most important objects to residents are often those that say something about themselves—whether they tell a narrative of the past, or relate to significant relationships, or indeed serve to replicate their own offline lives. Some of following narratives emerged in the conversation space of a discussion we initiated on the SL forums or were initiated by forum participants themselves. Our own forum thread was entitled "Objects of the Dead," and this theme is reflected in the responses of residents. Madelaine shared her story in this context, and her response demonstrates the interplay of RL and SL relationships as well as objects of intergenerational memory, attachment, and custodianship in the formulation of SL lives. Madelaine incorporated the unusual "monster door" of her childhood bedroom into her SL home. Her avatar wears a pocket watch modelled after a family heirloom

[8] David S. Kirk and Abigail Sellen, "On Human Remains: Values and Practice in the Home Archiving of Cherished Objects," *ACM Transactions on Computer-Human Interaction* 17, no. 3 (July 1, 2010): 17, https://doi.org/10.1145/1806923.1806924.

[9] Peter Nagy and Bernadett Koles, "'My Avatar and Her Beloved Possession': Characteristics of Attachment to Virtual Objects: CHARACTERISTICS OF ATTACHMENT TO VIRTUAL OBJECTS," *Psychology & Marketing* 31, no. 12 (November 2014): 1122–35, https://doi.org/10.1002/mar.20759.

which was handed down from her grandfather to her father and her own father to her. She wrote that

> There's nothing in my SL inventory to memorialize anyone or anything that happened here. I do wear a broken SL pocket watch like the RL one passed down from my great grandfather to my father to me, and I did have a Monster Door in my skybox reminiscent of the one at the bottom of a wall in my RL childhood bedroom. Those are more expressions of a way of seeing the world that was passed down to me than a memorial to those who passed it. If I have a sentimental object in SL, it's Maddy. If I have a sentimental object in RL, it's me. The way I am is, I hope, reflective of all those who've affected me over the years. It's a lot more fun to channel old friends than just be reminded of them.

In RL and SL Maddy understands her subjectivity as an incorporation and performative channelling of family and friends. She does not engage with the idea of memory objects as static things housed in SL inventories or lived spaces but rather sees value in channelling others and keeping them alive through her avatar. However, this channelling is not necessarily a matter of choice nor is it question of individual agency but is rather the very presence of others in making the self as a corpus of identifications, mostly unconscious, with significant others. If we imagine the embodied self as crypt of the living and dead, then it is made up of the genetic and mimetic repositories of generations.[10] The digital body of SL could indeed replicate these mimetic and genetic histories of generational inheritance not just at the level of an avatar image but in scripts of gestures and mannerisms and in how one speaks and writes in communication with others.

Madelaine's use of SL presents a challenge to the anonymity otherwise offered in SL. As Margaret has written elsewhere:

> In the *End of Absence*, Michael Harris signals the passing of a generation whose biography began outside computers and digital media networks. This is a generation in which digital things—the stuff of the Internet, emails, mobile phones and their internal data—have little or no deep biographical or mnemonic significance. This is a dying generation, and a dying way of life where the physical photograph, contained in the photograph album,

[10] Margaret Gibson, "Bodies without Histories," *Australian Feminist Studies* 21, no. 49 (March 1, 2006): 51–63, https://doi.org/10.1080/08164640500470644.

> contained in the home, was a customary practice of shared memory making and dwelling with the memories and images of others.[11]

In some ways SL simulates a pre-internet life in the capacity to remain anonymous and to set up a life disconnected from the integration of diverse roles, audiences, and relationships that now converge within and across the life integration on social media platforms. It is increasingly difficult to compartmentalise one's life, keeping different audiences and relationships separate.[12] It also difficult to just take leave of one's past, disconnect from past relationships, and make a fresh start. While past lives may continue in memory and material culture, this is different from the agency of social media to find and reunite us with our old school peers and former work colleagues and rebind us to our past selves and lives. Like moving to a new city or a different country, SL offers a discrete, fresh start life in a digital world context. Madelaine's narrative, however, demonstrates that some residents nonetheless wish to bring their existing life with them as they make this fresh start. Her decision to replicate objects associated with family and childhood suggests a type of commitment to continuity in terms of her identity and narrative of self. Just as a person moving to a new country may bring with them mementoes of a previous life, Madelaine transferred these significant markers of her personal history to her new virtual life.

Madelaine's passage into SL is also marked by a trajectory of loss. In a relationship in another virtual world context, Madelaine had hoped that her partner would follow her into SL. Instead, he got married in RL and left their relationship. He later died in RL. Madelaine brought this former partner who was deceased in RL back to a virtual life world and into the second life that he never had with her. He is an alt that she activates and which concomitantly recognises his earlier loss to her and the loss to life both real and virtual, while it also constitutes a mode of recuperation:

> Snugs is the last vestige of an online friendship I had with a fella long before coming to SL. I thought he might like it here, and so I created an avatar for him. He was a softy with a gruff exterior. I named his avatar "Snugs Eisenhart" as a tease. Rather than follow me into SL, he got married. He passed away a few years later, followed by his wife. When I returned to SL

[11] Margaret Gibson, "What We Leave behind," *New Philosopher*, November 2017, 78.

[12] Alice E. Marwick and danah boyd, "I Tweet Honestly, I Tweet Passionately: Twitter Users, Context Collapse, and the Imagined Audience," *New Media & Society* 13, no. 1 (February 2011): 114–33, https://doi.org/10.1177/1461444810365313.

> after a brief hiatus, I resurrected Maddy and Snugs, both as McMasters. The banter you see between them is much like that between that old friend and me, my late Father and me, Mom and me … between anyone I hold dear and me.

By resurrecting her SL avatar and creating an avatar of her deceased ex-partner in SL, Maddy has created an afterlife in which they are together. The deceased is living on through Maddy as a roleplay character who engages in banter. However, this relationship of Maddy and Snugs is also mediated by the bantering style of other significant relationships—"my late Father and me, Mom and me." This is an example of the creative kinship which exists everywhere but which becomes recognisable through narrative. This act of storytelling gives a sense of narrative to understood truths about family histories and ways of communicating. Maddy understands that her SL is a habitus of familiar ways of being formed and shared with significant others both on- and offline. Furthermore, this post like many others shows the interplay and flow into SL of childhood memories of home and the objects that defined that time and place, leaving a mark in memory. SL enables residents to reconnect with childhood memorabilia and the things that made up that everyday lifeworld. While the biblical mantra bids us to "put away childish things," as we grow up that does not mean that they disappear or go away without a trace. Indeed, things or objects have their own agency and can find a way back into conscious memory and futures of meaning and value, often despite ourselves.

Objects of Memory

Photographs mark time. They show the body, represent it, and show too the moment in time at which a photograph is taken.[13] Photographs taken in SL are digital—digital representations of a digital world. They rarely move outside the computer screen. The bodies they represent are bodies unmarked by time in the way we understand such concepts when speaking of the physical body. Yet they too demonstrate temporal markers specific to SL. Not only do they depict places and people who may no longer be present, but they also depict the state of advancement of SL in terms of graphics, possibilities for creation, and options for self-expression at the

[13] Margaret Gibson, "Melancholy Objects," *Mortality* 9, no. 4 (November 2004): 290, https://doi.org/10.1080/13576270412331329812.

time they are taken. The difference is not between one body which is youthful and one which shows physical age—it is between one youthful body and another made possible by different graphical technologies. These previous forms of embodiment which become obsolete are kept through photographs.

The power of photographs in SL is therefore to recall not just the self or the other who has been and is no longer, and not just the place which is gone, but an entire mode of experience which is no longer possible—for which one ostensibly ought not yearn because it has been replaced with an updated, improved version—but through which one may have experienced many significant moments. The power of these images to recall previous selves—and the level of meaning which may be ascribed to such selves—was demonstrated by a couple we encountered in our study. Samantha and Louis met in SL and were later married offline. SL was an important part of the trajectory and narrative of their relationship, and a year after their marriage, Louis sought to recognise that fact through tattooing a replica of a photograph he had taken in SL of their avatars together (Fig. 5.1). The avatars thus memorialised have long since altered to the point of being unrecognisable. The tattoo captures a specific moment in the trajectory of their relationship, in the history of their representations of self through the medium of the avatar, and also in SL's own history. The decision to record the image in this way highlights the relevance of the avatars, as well as the photographs, as objects of memory. It also transforms Louis's arm into an object of memory itself, part of a body which will be marked by time but which itself is the carrier of remembered timeless bodies rendered obsolete by the advancement of technology. Here the digital flesh becomes embedded in and inseparable from the physical flesh.

Previous studies have found similar acts of preserving old forms of technology and digital artefacts as sentimental objects. Kirk and Sellen, in a study of archived objects in the home, found that one couple who had met online and later formed a physical relationship kept the digital remnants of that earlier form of connection. These included saved emails and digital "gifts" such as e-cards and artworks.[14] The preservation of digital remainders even after a relationship transforms into a physical one is thus a practice with a storied history.

[14] "On Human Remains," 13.

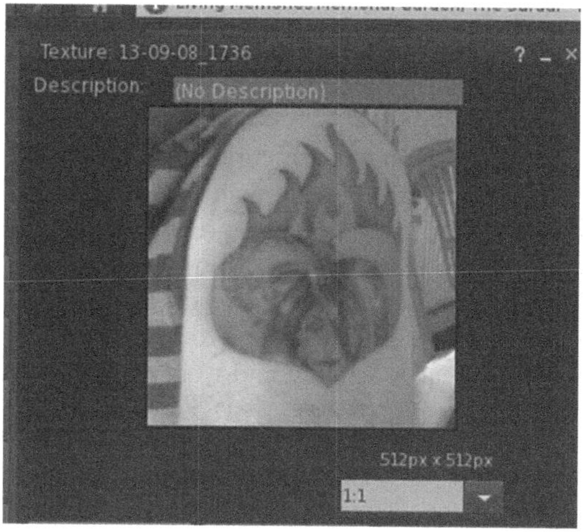

Fig. 5.1 Photograph of Louis's tattoo

Digital mementos have been described as less significant than physical ones. In addition, they have been described as quite limited in scope, with the notion of a digital memento generally referring to a photograph or video.[15] In SL, however, the boundary between digital and physical is in a sense blurred by the presence of the avatar, a digital self which is nonetheless an embodied self. The avatar mediates the relationship between digital object and physically embodied self, providing a means through which the object can be held, touched, or moved. Objects become meaningful because of their interplay with life and memory. The digital objects of memory held dear by SL residents can thus obtain significance in much the same way as physical reminders of significant people, places, and events. In a forum discussion in 2012, Margaret asked if virtual objects are just as emotionally or symbolically valuable as things in the world, and while many participants rejected this notion, one participant spoke about the value of her digital artwork and archive. Her narrative was unusual in the primacy given to the digital:

> Some of my works—even long before I came to sl—are digital and they hold a tremendous amount of value for me. Not just because of what they are,

[15] Daniela Petrelli and Steve Whittaker, "Family Memories in the Home: Contrasting Physical and Digital Mementos," *Personal and Ubiquitous Computing* 14, no. 2 (February 2010): 153–69, https://doi.org/10.1007/s00779-009-0279-7.

> but also because of what they represent, the feelings and emotions they bring about and even how they came to be in the first place. I don't expect anyone else to agree or even understand.

The memory and therapeutic work of the digital archive as a record of affective histories of feeling and emotion extends for this SL resident into using digital technologies to reproduce the personal items of childhood and adulthood. The translation of the physical object into a digital form and space does not, for this forum participant, diminish its value, rendering it secondary. The capacity to touch is also not privileged but rather the story of their becoming, and what they represent is the rubric of value:

> I have digital versions of some very personal things in sl, as well as elsewhere on the www. Things I've recreated from my childhood, from less happy times in my life, from happier times in my life even. Things I've recreated from the days when my children were younger-which really aren't too far off, my kids aren't too old, lol. They are very real to me. Not because I can physically touch them, but because of how they came to be, and what they represent. Others may laugh, and disagree with my thoughts on the matter, but i don't mind. I'm not ashamed that non-physical items hold such value for me. In fact, in some cases, I'm rather proud that these things can invoke such feelings, ones that at least at one time, were quite hidden.

The idea that hidden emotions came alive through the digital replica seems counterintuitive to the conventions of value ordering. This is a specific story of hidden emotions coming alive and being realised as if for the first time in the digital replica. The remaking has a capacity to illuminate what was once hidden and thus bring something potentially unrealised at the time into cognitive recognition or feeling. This is very much a therapeutic account suggesting perhaps more than it tells. In SL digital objects are valued in the work and skill required to translate and recreate a physical thing from its representation of time, place, circumstance, and relationships. It is the act of making digital mementoes and the idea that memory is about making and doing that is foremost in this and other narratives of this chapter. Also notable is the way some SL residents have migrated from former MMOs and brought with them the memory traces of their friends as well objects belonging their previous avatar game or social world lives.

In the 2017 forum discussion "Digital Objects of the Dead," participants described many kinds of mementoes, some of which are connected to the real life death of residents and their memory traces. As digital mementoes are the only materiality in which memories are made in SL, it stands to reason that they will be primary in this context. In other words, the physical does not pose a relational comparison if it is not relevant to the formation of memory and relational attachment in the first place.

Most residents we interviewed told us that their digital objects were less meaningful to them than their physical objects. To lose clothing, a book, or an item of furniture in SL was not to experience the same loss as if the same object had been owned physically and was taken away. Despite this, their emphasis on the reality of SL, and the way in which certain objects became reminders of particular significant people, suggests that some specific objects can become markers of memory.

Objects which have been crafted by or for a significant person are often the most meaningful. Artworks in particular have a special status as a privileged form of self-expression and thus an entry to the soul of self or other. One resident held as deeply significant an artwork created by a former lover of Sisyphus pushing a boulder up a hill. It is a large, grey work which took up much of the large display room in which it was situated. Leading up to Sisyphus is a series of human forms, representing the growth from childhood to adulthood. The artwork represents the pain which comes at the end of an easy life—the difficulty which the artist believed faced those who did not make challenging, difficult choices while they lived. It was the artist's representation of his own life, ending with what he knew to be a battle he could not win—with cancer. This work became an important marker of the deceased's life and outlook on its end. It also became a remainder of the relationship and the shared joys of giver and receiver, both of whom had viewed SL as a place in which they could be free, adventurous, and creative.

Objects which represent a relationship that has changed, even if it has not ended, can also become sentimental. While Samantha and Louis met in SL, Louis no longer visits the virtual world. During the early stages of their online relationship, Louis gave Samantha some jewellery. She has now made these items of jewellery part of her default appearance in SL. In doing so, she has ensured that, even though Louis is no longer an active participant in her digital life, he remains a continuous presence. Just as Louis wrote their relationship onto his physical body with his tattoo, Samantha has embedded it into her digital body through jewellery.

Replication

Our first base in SL was a Linden Home. This is a type of home which is provided to all residents who purchase a paid subscription. It was standardised, and, while it could be furnished, it could not be altered in any significant way. We felt very little impulse to decorate it in such a way as to make it appear "homey." Instead, we filled it with basic furniture. After a few months, we desired to create a space which was more welcoming to interviewees and, indeed, more pleasant for ourselves. Clara Coates purchased land and a cottage. In doing so, she sought to make a comfortable space replete with multiple sitting areas, a cosy nook, bookshelves, and ornaments. One of the first things she did was to seek out virtual pets. Clarissa, the typist behind Clara Coates, does not have pets in her own home and has not done so for several years. However, pets were always an important part of her family when she was growing up. She purchased a golden retriever and an orange tabby cat. Both were animated, semi-autonomous creatures which could walk, take naps, and be patted. It was only when naming them that she recognised the significance of the cat she had chosen. A fluffy orange tabby, it was a near replica to a beloved childhood pet, Scruffy. It is a matter of family legend that Scruffy hated children until Clarissa's mother became pregnant with her. During her pregnancy, however, he began nesting, and after her birth he was protective and loving towards her. Scruffy was the first significant pet in Clarissa's life, and to find herself, as avatar, unconsciously replicating him in her efforts to construct a welcoming home in SL was a shock. Clara Coates named our virtual cat "Scruff."

This experience suggests that the replication of significant offline objects and beings can occur unintentionally, a feature of the way in which a broad concept such as "home" is understood and experienced. Some replication, of course, is absolutely intentional. There is an important connection between replication and nostalgia, and the next chapter will explore the narratives of two women whose nostalgic yearning for home led them to recreate spaces of memory for their mothers. However, the replication of pets, as occurred in the setting up of our home, appears to be common. In response to a query we posted on the SL forums, one respondent stated that her most significant object in SL was her cat, which was a virtual representation of the RL cat with which she lived.

Objects of the Dead

Human existence and experience are inherently transitional. In a physical sense, the body serves as a reminder of this transitionality and the fragility of human being and living. While the physical body is marked by age and illness, the avatar body, unless by specific design, is not. Despite this, the avatar is dependent upon the user. While mortality is not visible in the embodiment of the avatar, it becomes an important part of the material culture of SL through the rules relating to the objects of those who have died.

Linden Lab only allows for objects of the deceased to be provided to loved ones in very limited circumstances. They provided an official guide on the subject which states that:

> In your will, you must include the legal (real life) name of the person who you want to inherit your Second Life account and assets in the event of your death.
>
> Pursuant to Section 4.1 of our Terms of Service:
>
> You may not sell, transfer or assign your Account or its contractual rights, licenses and obligations, to any third party (including, for the avoidance of doubt, permitting another individual to access your Account) without the prior written consent of Linden Lab.[16]

In many circumstances, this would represent an insurmountable boundary. Residents may not necessarily be connected to their loved ones in a way which makes it possible for them to be aware of their legal names. They may also not be aware of the requirement to receive written permission from Linden Lab or may not be able to obtain such permission. Even where a person is able to leave their account to a loved one in their will—something we have not encountered in our research—Linden Lab requires a significant amount of evidence, including a copy of the death certificate and a copy of the will, in order to provide the transfer.

It is likely that most transferrals are arranged privately, outside the knowledge of Linden Lab and without adhering to the official rules. This can only occur where a resident feels comfortable providing another

[16] This official guide has since been removed from Second Life Wiki. Linden Labs, "Linden Lab Official: Death and Other Worries Outside Second Life," February 12, 2016, http://wiki.secondlife.com/wiki/Linden_Lab_Official:Death_and_other_worries_outside_Second_Life.

resident, or an intermediary, with their account credentials. Some residents have told us that they have provided close friends or siblings with their account details—others have saved credentials on their computers in order to enable loved ones to log in in the event of their death. The commonality here is that these means of preserving and allocating the online belongings of the deceased favour those they know and are related to offline.

This allocation of the belongings of the deceased mimics that which would occur offline. It raises the possibility of family digging through the virtual belongings of a resident after their passing, keeping or discarding according to their own value judgements. The entirety of an account, indeed, may be discarded as unimportant. A second life could be reduced, in the perception of those left with the power to make decisions, to a mere game. The possibility of those empowered to dispose of the belongings of the deceased misinterpreting their significance—or interpreting their significance differently to other key stakeholders—is of course not limited to SL. The key difference here is the likelihood that those to whom the objects have most meaning—those who are likely to associate specific objects with a significant other—will not be those who are empowered to dispose of those objects. The potential result of this is complete erasure. If a resident logs off for the final time without making arrangements for the fate of their digital possessions, they may disappear completely. Not only their avatar, but also their home, their clothes, and their creations would be rendered permanently absent from the virtual world.

Alternatively, offline loved ones may improperly dispose of the digital possessions of the deceased. Margaret has previously highlighted the moral imperative felt by many family members not to profit from the death of their deceased. Significant objects, particularly clothes, are kept, given to loved ones, or donated to charity.[17] In SL, however, we have encountered instances of family members who have not followed this unwritten rule. Laura, who ran an art gallery with her SL partner Elliott, had access to his account. However, Elliott gave his account details to his RL wife and son and did not leave detailed instructions for his possessions. This led to a difficult situation:

> Elliott was a bit messy, RL and SL and I never really thought about it. I had the password of his avi and he told me I could use it. I already did when he

[17] Margaret Gibson, *Objects of the Dead: Mourning and Memory in Everyday Life* (Carlton, Vic.: Melbourne University Press, 2008).

> was ill now and then to pay the rent of the sim [on which their art gallery was situated]. But he apparently also gave his password before he died to his son and wife. And his son then logged in. His wife thought she could be rich selling Elliott's art. The idea hahahaha. SL art won't make you rich. It only costs money to have a gallery. Anyway I have some of his art but yes we should have thought about this and transferred stuff. Oh well, life goes on and nothing is forever. Certainly not in SL. It's a fast world.

While Laura was disappointed that she was not able to retain Elliott's artworks, her primary response was one of amusement and disdain for his wife's behaviour in attempting to profit from his death. This decision was seen as demonstrating a lack of connection to and understanding of the SL context in which these artworks were created. Laura was already in possession of a few significant artworks and had documented all of Elliott's work through photographs. For her the loss of these objects was not as significant as the disconnection revealed in the way in which they were lost. In attempting to make a profit from the sale of Elliott's art, his wife revealed that she did not understand the social realities of his virtual life.

Often, when a resident dies in RL, there will be no one left behind who has access to their account details. In such instances the likely outcome is that their belongings will simply disappear. Occasionally, however, serendipitous circumstances will lead to the preservation of a significant and important belonging. Michael was the co-owner of a sim which replicated key aspects of New Orleans. The sim was owned by a group, consisting of himself and a friend, to which he financially contributed. This meant that, as long as his friend continued paying for the land, it could exist without his contribution. However, he had the right to place objects on the land, and they could be left there even if he was not logged in to SL. One of the most significant SL items Michael possessed was Twist the dog. This was an animated, semi-autonomous dog which was programmed to respond to commands from any nearby avatar. Twist requires and responds to affectionate acts such as being patted or cuddled.

Like the countless users of Tamagotchis or Neopets in their heyday, Michael loved his digital pet. Twist went everywhere with him. When Michael died, Twist was outside his inventory, freely roaming his home. Like many other items—such as furniture or houses—the dog could, once spawned, continue to exist in-world despite its owner not being logged into his account. Twist remains a beloved and significant presence in Michael's former home. Michael's friend regularly rents land to new residents, and on every occasion they are introduced to Twist. The dog wanders freely into the homes and shops of residents and is a beloved fixture of the community. He is an enduring reminder of Michael's significance to that community—one that has outlived him and in some senses mediates a relationship between Michael and those residents who have moved into the community of which he was once an integral member.

Such serendipity cannot be relied upon. When Edmund's brother Sam died, he believed that he would be able to continue accessing some of Sam's creations. Sam had been a prolific builder, and his works were on display in a large sim where they lived together. Sam had set the permissions on some of these items so that Edmund could alter or take them. In the immediate aftermath of Sam's death, Edmund did not feel emotionally prepared to visit these sentimental objects and remove them.

> I had permissions to take Sam's items, so I told myself I wanted to get copies of as many builds as I could. But I couldn't handle it that night, so I put it off until the next day, and that was a mistake. The other person who knew him in RL had land rights to where we had been living, a full sim and a homestead together, and I had just logged in when I got the message that a whole bunch of stuff had been returned to me. In his own grief, this guy had wiped the sims.

This action could not be undone. It was immediate, irreparable, and devastating. Edmund described his immediate response and the response of Sam's other loved ones:

> It felt like what was left of him was ripped away from me, I won't lie. I was so angry I had to walk away from the computer and take a walk. [This was a] friend, not somebody I had met more than in passing, oddly. But other people in SL got wind of it and said some very firm things to him. [Sam's] SL lover, who was going to meet him later that year, even tried getting into his SL account but couldn't.

The loss of these objects was upsetting to Edmund. However, he positioned his distress in relation of others who were viewed as having a right to be upset or to grieve the loss of these significant objects. Sam's lover—not described as a boyfriend or a partner because of the specific master-slave relationship within the Gor community—was, in Edmund's eyes, a person who was particularly wronged by the destruction of Sam's creations. This speaks to the enduring special position of partners within SL hierarchies of loss. It also, however, speaks to the lack of power partners may have in determining the fate of significant objects after a death in SL. This is in keeping with the lack of power partners whose relationships do not fit into normative, particularly heteronormative, structures often experience after a significant death. Bent and Magilvy interviewed lesbian women and found that in many cases a lack of support led to a lack of resolution of their grief. This could occur through being engaged in legal battles, for example, over the objects of the deceased, or through a lack of recognition from family members.[18] In asserting Sam's lover's right to access his belongings after his death, Edmund is rewriting these hierarchies into a form which recognises the romantic partner as valid and important, even in the absence of a legally or broadly socially recognised relationship.

The ease with which SL objects can be deleted, then, contributes to the risk that a more immediate erasure will occur than would be possible in the physical world. While it is possible that a person dealing with the physical belongings of a deceased loved one may be too quick to discard, or too destructive in their grief, and live to regret the loss of significant object markers which would serve to represent the lost loved one in the world, this process is rarely as simple as the click of a button. It is also rarely a process which can occur without the consent of those whose relationships were most clearly socially recognised. The potential for an object to be owned, edited, and deleted by multiple people in SL undoes some of these distinctions. Sam's friend received significant social censure for his impulsive act of grief. He lost key connections in the Gorean community. Edmund found his explanation unconvincing but attempted to reach out and repair some of the damage:

> He said that he couldn't stand to see those things there, so he wiped the land. That just didn't make a lot of sense since he owned a land company with over 200 sims; he could have just gone somewhere else. I wrote him about six months later and told him that I forgave him, and that I wondered if he could possibly help me find some land to keep some [Sam's remaining buildings] on and I got a very terse reply and haven't seen or heard from him since.

[18] Katherine N. Bent and J. Kathy Magilvy, "WHEN A PARTNER DIES: LESBIAN WIDOWS," *Issues in Mental Health Nursing* 27, no. 5 (January 2006): 447–59, https://doi.org/10.1080/01612840600599960.

In other cases, those with the power to control objects belonging to those who have died, rather than destroying them or allowing them to remain unchanged, choose to revitalise those objects as a means of perpetuating the memory of the deceased. In one of the tiny community's most populous sims, there is a shop called Hippo. It once belonged to a clothing designer whose avatar was a small, pink, hippo. She would sell her wares for profit in her store and in the SL Marketplace. After she died, her friends kept the store open but gave away all of the clothing for free. In this way they have ensured her legacy insofar as the designs of this resident continue to be present on members of the tiny community. We have been unable to trace the person who has enacted this work of memory. The story has been obtained through notecards and signage in the store itself. The lack of available information about those who have done the work of memorialisation perhaps unintentionally allows the clothes, and the store, to stand on their own—as though they were waiting for an owner who will never return.

Objects in SL have their own lives dependent on, but often detached from, those who create and own them. The creation of items—for one's own use or for commercial gain—has long been a heavily advertised means of using SL. Despite this, Linden Lab has not been able to construct guidelines that residents would view as satisfactory to enable virtual belongings to be passed on after the death of a resident. This is a serious failing. For those residents who have trusting relationships with significant others in-world, or, more commonly, have significant relationships outside of SL, there is the option of providing another individual with one's account credentials. This requires a level of trust which may not be easily mustered, and an ability to continue to keep the holder of these details abreast with any changes to passwords or email addresses. It also requires that the giver believes that their belongings will be maintained and allocated as they would wish.

The nature of items in SL is such that they can be destroyed, without trace, in an instant. Thus, even though as digital objects they are stored outside a single physical space and are theoretically—if not actually—immune to natural disasters, theft, and decay, SL objects have their own unusual level of fragility. A single act of destructive grief can erase the entirety of the objects left behind by someone who has died. That such an action can be taken—and that an action of this kind is likely to lead to serious pain and distress on the part of loved ones—potentially speaks to a flaw in SL itself and a lack of recognition on the part of its designers of the significance that people, relationships, and indeed objects could carry within this virtual world.

The problem of digital remains is one that resonates outside of SL. It is an issue which must be grappled with by social media sites, video sharing sites, and indeed such spaces as forums where users may be anonymous. The question of how a company is to determine that a person has died, and what should be done with the markers that have been left behind, is a central problem of our modern epoch. Engaging philosophically with moral status of digital remains, Stokes argues that "these artefacts in fact enjoy a claim to moral regard akin to that of corpses".[19] Our digital footprints seem to offer us a kind of immortality. Too often, we fail to think of the fragility of the actual objects that make up this footprint and the uncertainty of their fate once we are no longer present to manage them.

[19] Patrick Stokes, "Deletion as Second Death: The Moral Status of Digital Remains," *Ethics and Information Technology* 17, no. 4 (December 2015): 237–48, https://doi.org/10.1007/s10676-015-9379-4.

CHAPTER 6

Nostalgia

Introduction

SL is filled with nostalgia for places and experiences residents have known, nostalgia for lost moments in SL's own history, and nostalgia for times and places that never existed in quite their imagined form. In this respect, perhaps, it is no different to the world offline. It is different, however, in the scope an average person has to recreate the longed-for moments and spaces and to do so in a form that reflects how they are viewed in memory rather than how they were or could have been in reality. Nostalgia is traditionally associated with melancholy, including a sense that the world in which one lives is somehow alien in relation to an actual or imagined past.[1] The word, in fact, comes to us from medicine, where nostalgia was considered a treatable illness. But the notion of nostalgia as an illness is, as Starobinski[2] argues, part of the medicalised pathologisation of human emotions that existed more freely as part of the human condition before diagnostic scrutiny and disease classification. The medicalisation of nostalgia is also true of the history of grief that has gained pathological forms in psychiatric literature and, in more recent history, had a more hidden status under the medical diagnostic rubric of depression. Starobinski's history of

[1] Bryan S Turner, "A Note on Nostalgia," *Theory, Culture & Society* 4 (1987): 149.

[2] Jean Starobinski and William S. Kemp, "The Idea of Nostalgia," *Diogenes* 14, no. 54 (1966): 81–103.

M. Gibson, C. Carden, *Living and Dying in a Virtual World*,
Palgrave Macmillan Memory Studies,
https://doi.org/10.1007/978-3-319-76099-5_6

the idea of nostalgia shows it to be a symptom prevalent with conditions of war in other people's territories and with the expansion of colonial and imperial projects of Western countries to unfamiliar, unhomely places. Nostalgia as the idea of "homesickness" then is part of the mobility characterising Western modernity to include both voluntary and involuntary forms of human movement, creating a love and longing for a return to home.

For Boym, nostalgia in more contemporary times has become a historical emotion linked to time—a longing for a different time and thus beyond a spatial geography in the form of longing for home or homelands. In this sense it can be understood as a rebellion against the onward march of time and a desire to experience time as one does place, allowing desired moments to be revisited.[3] Turner identifies four dimensions of the nostalgic paradigm as used in social and cultural discourses. The first is a sense of historical decline in relation to a lost period of time. The second is a perceived absence of moral certainty and personal wholeness. The third is a sense of lost individual freedoms and the disappearance of genuine social relationships. Finally, he identifies the fourth dimension as a perceived loss of "simplicity, personal authenticity and emotional spontaneity."[4] He argues that particular cultures, including former colonies and colonisers, appear to be particularly prone to crises of nostalgia.[5]

Tannock states that nostalgia itself is often evaluated negatively in scholarly discourse but argues that critiques of nostalgia are often in fact critiques of the content, author, and audience of particular nostalgic narratives. Nostalgia itself, as a positive evaluation of the past in relation to the present, has, he argues, the potential to create progressive or enabling narratives.[6] For Pickering and Keightley, nostalgia is complicated, going beyond trivialised or sentimentalised yearnings for the past as evident in mass representations and advertising culture. Instead, nostalgia encompasses a range of responses to the past which cannot be understood in a dichotomous relationship with the work of the historian.[7] While endorsing

[3] Svetlana Boym, "Nostalgia and Its Discontents," *The Hedgehog Review* 9, no. 2 (2007): 7.

[4] "A Note on Nostalgia," 150–51.

[5] 153–54.

[6] Stuart Tannock, "Nostalgia Critique," *Cultural Studies* 9, no. 3 (October 1995): 454, https://doi.org/10.1080/09502389500490511.

[7] "The Modalities of Nostalgia," *Current Sociology* 54, no. 6 (November 2006): 926, https://doi.org/10.1177/0011392106068458.

criticism of nostalgia as diminishing or delimiting historical consciousness and potentially carrying particular ideological meanings, they suggest that this is not true of all nostalgia—nostalgia ought instead to be thought of as culturally and historically specific with a range of multiple meanings and functions.[8] As they write, "we are all prey to nostalgia, particularly where a vehicle of personal memory, such as a photograph or a dead parent or lost lover, may touch us emotionally."[9] Nostalgia, in their view, enables us to see the fragility in the relationship between past and present, and this can feasibly be used for progressive aims.[10]

Higson argues that, while modern nostalgia is strongly temporal, being a response to the distinction and tension between the present and the past, postmodern nostalgia is atemporal. That which is irrecoverable, for which one yearns, in modern nostalgia becomes attainable.[11] He describes the online proliferation of nostalgia for the recent past. The bittersweet aspect of modern nostalgia, in which the longed-for past cannot ever be reclaimed, is replaced by a nostalgia which is commodified and which is all sweet—which celebrates the past without wistfulness.[12] In modern nostalgia one longs for the past without returning to it, while in postmodern nostalgia it becomes possible to become one with the past. Experiences associated with the past can be relived, the wistfulness cured.[13] In SL the ability to relive the past, identified by Higson in relation to period films and nostalgic webpages, is amplified by the creative potential of the virtual world as a space for constructing and reconstructing remembered spaces—and of experiencing these spaces *as* spaces in which it is possible to live and move and re-enact aspects of the remembered or imagined past. The self can, in SL, be reconstructed as a self which matches the historical space in which one operates. Postmodern nostalgia goes beyond the remembered past. It also includes the longing for experiences, times, and places which have never been part of one's own biographical history except as ideas, sounds, and images of times past. We may think of the popularity of period dramas or the enduring draw of figures such as Marilyn Monroe who are

[8] 933–34.

[9] 935.

[10] 938.

[11] "Nostalgia Is Not What It Used to Be: Heritage Films, Nostalgia Websites and Contemporary Consumers," *Consumption Markets & Culture* 17, no. 2 (March 4, 2014): 125, https://doi.org/10.1080/10253866.2013.776305.

[12] 126.

[13] 128.

remembered fondly and reinterpreted long after their historical moment has passed. Nostalgia has been disconnected from lived history to become a longing or wish to be in a time and place where one has never been or could be. It is about possibilities closed, not by the onward march of time during one's own life but prior to birth. This relates not just to media cultures but also to intergenerational histories connected to inherited memories and stories of parents and grandparents and the places, things, and musical styles that made up their biographical time and place.

Nostalgia for Home

Nostalgia, in its original sense, meant homesickness—a yearning to inhabit the home or homeland of one's childhood—and this continues to be an important aspect of the contemporary phenomenon.[14] SL residents who possess the time and skills to do so are able to reconstruct the buildings or other spaces in which childhood was lived. One of our interviewees, Lorelai, told Margaret that she had reconstructed her childhood home in SL. This was the house in which she had grown up and in which she felt a distinct sense of belonging. Her parents had been unable to retain it and had sold the house in 1980.

Lorelai uses SL not only as a way to catch up with real-life friends and family, and importantly it is where she is able to spend time with her mother who geographically lives on the other side of the USA from her. In her 70s, her mother comes to visit her at her SL home, and they like to do the mother-daughter thing of going shopping together. While Lorelai sees her SL home as a "home base" for her mother's visits, she spoke about how she decided to build, as a gift for her mother's birthday, the family home of her [Lorelai's and her siblings'] childhood:

> I built my old house I grew up in RL .... I built it from memory and many times when I was stumped I would ring my mother [and] we would discuss it. I just built it the way I remembered. no certain age. i still have some things to do to the build. i want to furnish it. one day I will.

[14] Krystine Irene Batcho, "Nostalgia: The Bittersweet History of a Psychological Concept.," *History of Psychology* 16, no. 3 (2013): 165–76, https://doi.org/10.1037/a0032427; Kathy Hamilton et al., "Nostalgia in the Twenty-First Century," *Consumption Markets & Culture* 17, no. 2 (March 4, 2014): 101–4, https://doi.org/10.1080/10253866.2013.776303.

> I want the same furniture as then … it was a gift for one of her [mother's] birthdays to surprise her …. And she loved that house. I don't live in it now [in rl]. Mum and Dad had to sell it in 1980. I know mum missed it alot. We all did.

This is a story about the loss of the family home. There is a sense of shared loss—"I know mum missed it a lot. We all did," Lorelai says. She has used SL as a platform (in both senses of the word) in which to reconstruct that loss and bring a version of the remembered family home into existance. On her mother's birthday, Lorelai sent an invitation to the virtual address. Her mother just needed to click on it, and it would teleport her to the home located on a plot of land owned by Lorelai. There is a generational reversal with the daughter owning the land and giving back some version of the family home to the parent, her mother. There is something magical in this story, not just because it offers the fantasy and plays into the narrative of time travel, popular in SL, like other online social and game worlds. It is also magical because unlike the Freudian wish fulfilment taking place in the dream state, it is taking place in waking life. This story is also about an act of generosity in putting time and creative labour into making something come back to a second life that was valued and lost in first life. It is reversal of fortune that second life/SL was able to make first life more *tangibly real* through the virtuality of pixels.

Lorelai was waiting at the house to surprise her mother and show her around. The real-life family home of childhood was always already a virtual existence as a lost reality substituted by memory. SL became, then, a place in which to realise and reconstitute that loss in another virtual form. The act of reconstruction does not therefore recuperate the past but rather brings the passing of the past into a representational form. *It is the work of mourning*. This is the pathos in this narrative of a mother and grown daughter in their avatar embodiments ghost walking through the rooms of the family home brought back to some semblance of a life.

Lorelai's SL house was therefore a recreation constructed, over two decades after she last stepped foot in the building, entirely from memory. "I built it just the way I remembered," she said, "no certain age." Where she was unable to remember a specific detail, she sought information from her mother. The home may be understood as a means of addressing the wistfulness of nostalgia through mapping the memories of two generations of women into a physical, if virtual, space. While Lorelai retained possession of the house, she saw it as a birthday present for her mother, then 72, who would visit SL and spend time in Lorelai's other SL home. Her mother did not have her own SL home. "My base is always her base." The reconstructed family home was not created for them to live in SL but only visit and thus pass through. We do not know if they visited separately or together the reconstructed family home any other time other than that very first time where they walked together in the rooms and reminisced.

The nostalgic reconstruction of shared spaces of family memory arose in other interviews. Isabelle found that, when she began using SL, "I always wanted just a few more prims than I had so I would move to a larger and larger parcel until we got a homestead for our family." Isabelle's elderly mother and brother are both users of SL, and she found that, once she obtained a full sim, she could begin to reconstruct the spaces and memories of their times together offline. Her brother had moved to the opposite side of America, and her mother, who has Parkinson's disease, had been forced to give up her two holiday homes in Florida and the North Carolina mountains. The sim Isabelle created became a space in which the three of them could be together and her mother could enjoy the spaces and activities from which she had been separated by illness. In her family sim, Isabelle recreated her mother's Florida home and her summer cottage in the mountains. She reconstructed the camping areas they had loved before illness and separation rendered camping as a family impossible. She constructed hiking trails over the virtual mountains. "Everything that I put into that sim was very symbolic for our family," she said, "it was built with love."

The sim provided a space in which Isabelle, her mother, and her brother were able to spend time together in a form of playful community that geographical separation would have rendered otherwise impossible. In 2016 Isabelle's brother moved to live near herself and their mother. "He has said that would never have happened if not for SL," she told us. "Although we would have described ourselves as a close family, we lived on opposite sides of the country. In SL we were able to have experiences together which brought us closer." The family homestead was transformed into a public space in which people living with Parkinson's are invited to join together in a supportive community. The North Carolina cabin is still present, as are the interactive virtual pets Isabelle purchased for her family's use.

These two narratives highlight the extent to which differences in class and access to economic capital determine the way in which nostalgia for home is enacted in SL. Lorelai and Isabelle were motivated by similar intentions—reconstructing a lost and loved space for an elderly mother and creating a place to share with family—but the types of spaces they enacted, and their ability to do so, speak to vastly different class positions. Lorelai's parents had been unable to keep a loved family home—Isabelle's mother had lost, not her primary place of residence, but two properties she had obtained for the purposes of recreation. Lorelai's mother had suffered her loss due to financial hardship, where Isabelle's mother had experienced loss due to incapacity associated with age. The extent to which these daughters were able to recreate spaces of memory for their mothers also speaks to differences in resources. Lorelai constructed a house which, she told us, she had not yet been able to furnish. Isabelle was able to purchase an entire sim—something which requires not only an upfront payment but also an ongoing monthly maintenance fee of over $100USD. She was also able to afford the time to carefully and lovingly reconstruct remembered spaces on this land—something that she said took extensive free time over the course of a year. While it is possible, then, for the urge to return to a beloved place of personal memory to be met through the use of the tools available within SL, this does not correspond to a situation in which the ability to indulge these nostalgic urges is equally or democratically allocated. Rather, the way in which nostalgia is enacted has the potential to replicate not only the beloved space but also the class divides existing offline.

Nostalgia for Second Life's Own History

Tom Boellstorff writes that "[r]esidents of virtual worlds teach us that they are real places that must be understood in their own terms."[15] We find, in the nostalgia many residents feel and enact for the history of SL, a sense that not only is the virtual world a real place but also that its history is also a real history, deserving of respect and commemoration. In its most blatant sense, this nostalgia is enacted through visiting the monuments, put in place or preserved by Linden Labs, to former iterations of the virtual world. These include historic buildings such as Governor Linden's mansion, landmarks like the giant beanstalk, and a museum to the history of SL. Sloan, writing on nostalgia in video games, states that from the time

[15] "For Whom the Ontology Turns: Theorizing the Digital Real," *Current Anthropology* 57, no. 4 (August 2016): 395, https://doi.org/10.1086/687362.

of the seventh generation of video games (around 2005–2013), gaming communities became characterised, in part, by a nostalgia for gaming's own history.[16] Sloan indicates that games have begun to actively incorporate references to a range of media, including previous games, in order to satisfy the nostalgic urges of gaming communities. The preservation of spaces which speak to a former iteration of SL may be understood as practices which speak to the nostalgic urges of the SL community generally. We have found, however, that a nostalgic longing for past events and spaces is more broadly disseminated.

Kai Woodhouse is tall and slender. His Linden home, the standard 512-square metre house residents obtain for free with a premium account, is distinctively and stylishly decorated. Covering the back wall are photographs taken in SL itself. Photographs, Kai says, are one of the few categories of objects in SL to which he ascribes real-world value. The images on his wall were taken at various events—they include not just people but also places. Most of these no longer exist. In 11 years spent in SL, Kai has seen quite a few beloved spaces disappear. "As in life, it happens," he says, "I guess in RL entire places don't get deleted. But people come and go." This suggests the limits of enacting nostalgia within SL—while it is possible to recreate beloved spaces and objects of social and cultural memory, any resident who also engages in SL for an extended period of time will see beloved people, things, and places disappear. For long-term residents like Kai, photographs can be the only remainder.

SL residents often seem to chart their personal histories in terms of what they have been without: what new technological developments they have seen arrive. For instance, James, a museum curator, responded to a question about how long he had been in SL by stating that he remembered a time before poseballs were invented. These are the ubiquitous balls featuring animated scripts which allow residents to do anything from praying to engaging in sexual intercourse. Such temporal markers are a way of responding to the fact that SL is shaped by changes in technology in a way even the physical world is not. New advances have meant that the world can become more complicated. They have allowed for greater detail in textures, in furniture, and even in avatar design. Even the ability to hear another resident speak without opening an additional programme is a

[16] "Videogames as Remediated Memories: Commodified Nostalgia and Hyperreality in Far Cry 3: Blood Dragon and Gone Home," *Games and Culture* 10, no. 6 (November 2015): 526, https://doi.org/10.1177/1555412014565641.

technological advance—earlier in SL's history, sound was not available at all. These changes are therefore an important cultural touchstone for many residents—often one will meet a person who has retained outdated items due to their nostalgic appeal. This is despite the fact that such items often have a higher prim count and therefore have a detrimental impact on the total number of items that can be placed upon a particular piece of land. Such items are retained for sentimental, rather than practical, reasons.

Thus same nostalgic impulse, to reduce the space between the present and the past, is evident in the careful preservation of community histories. The tinies of Raglan Shire, a group that prides itself on being one of the oldest in the virtual world, host a museum of tiny history featuring posters from events occurring in years past. The community, which at the time of writing is celebrating its tenth anniversary, holds a yearly "birthday month" in April. They also hold themed events such as the annual Winterfest celebration, fashion shows, and Halloween events. The carefully designed posters for events past and present grace their webpage and the homes of many community members.

Other communities demarcate spaces which are to remain unchanged during periods of redesign or upheaval. Jeremiah is the leader of an ashram which was given to him by its previous owner upon his departure from SL. He has often felt torn between a sense of respect and longing for the ashram as it existed under its former leader and a desire to modernise. "I realised that he gave it to me to keep as a living entity and not a cemetery monument," he said, "so gradually I've changed the ashram except for one historical section with is clearly marked." In this way he maintains a connection to the past—including to the mentor whose departure sparked, he says, a period of mourning—while building a space for the community of the future.

Time Travel

Nostalgia is, in part, about memory—not necessarily a literal memory but an imaginative act of remembering and imagining the past. Higson writes that "[t]he process of remembering [...] is closely attached to a desire to return in thought or in fact to that earlier time—even while it is clear that such a return can only be a fantasy."[17] In SL it is possible to return—as

[17] "Nostalgia Is Not What It Used to Be," 123.

avatar and through technologies which are themselves deeply temporal and associated with our present moment in history—to an earlier historical period.

Tom Griffiths has described historians as "professional time travellers,"[18] an astute descriptor which may be fruitfully borrowed in order to describe the creators of SL's many historical sims. In writing history, Griffiths states:

> [O]ne must first amass the clay, the raw material of reality, building up the rough form, gathering much more than one can eventually keep. Then begins the careful paring away, the sculpting and moulding, the tweaking out of detail. The final reality emerges, and one could believe that it was always there, trapped in the clay, awaiting discovery and release.[19]

In SL the final reality emerges, not in the form of a published manuscript but in reconstructions—of space, of objects, of clothing—which can be used by residents to travel, through their avatars, to the studied period. The world builders, amateur time travellers to Griffiths' professionals, select the aspects of the period they wish to convey—often architecture and décor, sometimes also clothing (through enforcing dress codes) or sounds—and leave absent that which is undesirable or too difficult. Thus historical sims in SL are nostalgic in the sense of providing entry to an idealised and imagined version of the past.

Historical sims should also be understood as virtual tourist destinations. The notion of virtual tourism has been around since before it was a real possibility. It has been suggested as a sustainable alternative to physical mass tourism since at least the 1990s.[20] In SL it begins to show its real potential. 1920s Berlin is one of the most popular roleplaying sims in SL. Set in the Weimar Republic, the sim features realistic buildings, a strict dress code, and regular themed events.

This simulation aims to replicate, in intricate detail, the physical world of Berlin in the 1920s. The founder, Jo Yardley (we use her real avatar

[18] Tom Griffiths, *The Art of Time Travel: Historians and Their Craft*. (Collingwood: Schwartz Publishing Pty. Ltd, 2016), 15, http://public.eblib.com/choice/publicfullrecord.aspx?p=4419742.

[19] Griffiths, 16.

[20] E.g. Jean-Michel Dewailly, "Sustainable Tourist Space: From Reality to Virtual Reality?," *Tourism Geographies* 1, no. 1 (February 1999): 41–55, https://doi.org/10.1080/14616689908721293.

name as she is a public figure within the virtual world), performed extensive historical research in constructing streets, buildings, and even advertisements as similar as possible to those which would have existed in the real historical location. Construction is an ongoing process, and, even after seven years, new buildings and details continue to be added. Yardley states that she has no real-life connection to Berlin or to the 1920s in particular. She states that she has an interest in twentieth-century history and, when determining what sort of sim to build, found that the 1920s Berlin was popular. "You need a theme people will visit," she said. "The building is 99% my work, all the buildings and textures are mine. But the community of course was built by the people." Yardley describes the ability to time travel as a key part of the space's appeal.

The setting clearly speaks to other residents of the SL community. A thriving community exists within the simulation. The strict dress code precludes members of many subcultures from entering the space without altering their avatar appearance. Neither furries nor vampires are welcome in the space as their presence would interrupt the fantasy created. Child avatars, who are unwelcome in many sims, are permitted and indeed encouraged through the provision of a school. In order to ensure that residents are able to visit the simulation, Jo Yardley has collaborated with a number of designers to provide free period-appropriate clothing at the entrance to the sim. Once residents become more engaged within the sim, however, it is uncommon to continue using these free items. A roaring trade in realistic 1920s clothing—Yardley demands historical accuracy and will not allow, for example, flapper costumes with excessively short skirts—exists on the Second Life Marketplace.

Residents who choose to live within the 1920s Berlin Project have the opportunity to become more deeply engaged through renting apartments or taking on professional duties. There are a number of jobs available in the sim. There are also roleplaying groups. The 1920s Berlin Project has a police force, a dance troupe, and a criminal underground. It regularly advertises jobs such as secretarial roles. This is a space in which full second lives can be enacted. It is also a space in which roleplay facilitates a particular form of relationship-building and interaction which would appear dramatic or out of place elsewhere in the virtual world. Clara Coates attended an engagement party within the 1920s Berlin Project. While she was not, of course, privy to the private conversations which may have taken place between participants, she found that the public discussion resembled the type of dialogue which may take place in a period drama. Residents enquired after familial relationships based on surnames. They enquired after one another's partners and engaged in flirtatious gossip. The mother of the groom epitomised this dramatic flair, beginning her speech by noting that the groom's father had recently died, "but I am not the widow." The type of past enacted in this environment is therefore not one which directly replicates the historical past of Berlin in the 1920s but is instead one informed by more recent popular culture depictions of history. This is a space of nostalgia and historical learning, but it is equally a space of fantasy and play.

While Yardley emphasises that she has attempted to keep her recreation as close to the historical reality of the replicated space and time as possible, she admits that some alterations were necessary. The scale of some buildings had to be changed so that they would fit in the sim. Even in a virtual world, space is not infinite. Other limitations, such as limits set by Linden Labs on the number of prims a particular parcel of land can hold, similarly shaped the project. Additionally, as is perhaps to be expected in a world catering primarily to users in the USA, the language heard most often in 1920s Berlin is English.

But beyond these alterations, which are recognised and perhaps expected, there is something missing, something that shaped the historical Weimar Republic and which would lead to a later, darker era in Germany's history. No uniforms can be worn in 1920s Berlin without permission. Only members of officially sanctioned groups are seen wearing police or military attire. A message one encounters upon entering the sim states that this is due to the tense political situation. The political situation in 1920s Berlin is acknowledged then, but it is itself largely absent. The head of the sim's police force states that 1920s Berlin is an educational space and that long-time residents are often inspired by their experiences to research the Weimer Republic. He also states that some of the details—such as a poster advocating that citizens respect the mothers of Jewish soldiers who died in the First World War—ensure that residents are always aware of the fact that they are roleplaying a period between two major world wars. "The wars are always with us," he said, "but in the shadows." The design of this sim and its prohibition of possible signifiers or historical prefiguring of anti-Semitism, Nazi, and fascism is an acknowledged historical reality of the German/Berlin future that has already happened but is necessarily suspended time as a future within a sim locked into an unchanging time period.

The very purpose of the space—as an attractive and atmospheric place in which residents can enjoy indulging their nostalgia and enacting glamorous 1920s identities—ensures that the political reality of Berlin in the 1920s must indeed remain "in the shadows." For context, Hitler gave one of his most famous speeches, on anti-Semitism, in August of 1920.[21] Even the poster mentioned above makes sense only in the historical context wherein the 1920s was a period during which Jewish soldiers became understood in racialised terms as "other."[22] The late 1920s were the time in which the Nazi Party began the political mobilisation which would position them as a viable political party.[23] This context, particularly the Nazi context, is erased in the SL iteration of 1920s Berlin.

None of this is to downplay the astounding beauty and architectural accuracy of Jo Yardley's creation. It is, as another resident told us, "a marvel." Instead, we wish to draw attention to the decontextualised nature of SL time travel which cannot, by its very nature, carry or reveal the layers of meaning inherent in the historical space and time being recreated. These recreated spaces are in fact spaces outside of time, which cannot be reconciled, however accurate they may be, with an actual historical moment. Despite this, they can be valuable, both in terms of promoting and preserving communities and in terms of promoting historical knowledge and understanding. But they can also perhaps sanitise and contribute to moral amnesia and wilful denial.

There is no coherence politically, geographically, and historically in SL—it has many historical periods and practices of time and travel and it has forms of politics that span left and right, to include extremes—although these spectrums are increasingly less intelligible in contemporary global politics. It has groups dedicated to Nazi propaganda, sado-masochism, and other death cults. This larger context creates the need for boundaries of access and roleplay in terms of how sims such as Berlin in the 1920s can morally operate. And yet, it is difficult not to feel some ambivalence about

[21] Claus-Christian W. Szejnmann, "Nazi Economic Thought and Rhetoric During the Weimar Republic: Capitalism and Its Discontents," *Politics, Religion & Ideology* 14, no. 3 (September 2013): 360, https://doi.org/10.1080/21567689.2013.820436.

[22] Tim Grady, "Creating Difference: The Racialization of Germany's Jewish Soldiers after the First World War," *Patterns of Prejudice* 46, no. 3–4 (July 2012): 318–38, https://doi.org/10.1080/0031322X.2012.701802.

[23] Anders G. Kjøstvedt, "The Dynamics of Mobilisation: The Nazi Movement in Weimar Berlin," *Politics, Religion & Ideology* 14, no. 3 (September 2013): 338–54, https://doi.org/10.1080/21567689.2013.820433.

a sim dedicated to this era despite the measures to contain its internal cultural and political dynamics.

The Old Time Radio Room is precisely what the name would suggest. It is a room, decorated in an indistinct "retro" style, which, at designated times, hosts a group of people who visit to listen to radio shows from the past. The room has been running, in various forms, for seven years. It is therefore imbued with nostalgia both for the past in the sense of mid-twentieth-century popular culture and SL's own past. Its owner, Klopstick Sandalwood (as with Jo Yardley, we use Klopstick's real avatar name as this is inextricable from his work), is a history buff who describes the room as the culmination of an experiment:

> I was interested in finding out if I could build a group of people here around a rather obscure shared interest. This all got its start at a place called the USO Hangar, where they had WW2 era music and a USO dance. A lot of people came for the music, but didn't have a lot of context for it, other than maybe "My father/grandfather was in WW2, and I think the music is a lot of fun."
>
> I've studied a lot of history, and know the era well (and my dad was a WW2 vet), so I added bits of trivia and fun information about the era in my conversation during the dances. People seemed to enjoy learning more, which was very gratifying. I've been an old time radio show fan for a long, long time, well prior to my time in SL. And I thought maybe I could stream some of the old shows for people for some fun and as a way to give them more context for the USO stuff. We set up in the loft of the hangar, very basic—just some couches and a rug and a couple of pictures of the Andrews Sisters and Bing Crosby on the walls and I learned to do the streaming stuff by hit or miss.
>
> Well, an amazing thing happened. We had a small cadre of people at the first show and it was a big hit. I think it was some of the Lux Theater shows, which were radio versions of the popular motion pictures of the day, done by the same actors and actresses. There was intense concentration during the shows, and people started asking about all kinds of things. A lot of it was about references that were being made in the show, things they didn't get, or the political/war situation on that date. And the other thing that happened was that people started "talking back" to the show in chat. You know the kind of thing, "Oh no! Don't open that closet! He's *in* there!!!" It had a wonderfully cozy and happy atmosphere. Word started to get around, and the crowd got bigger. We had some who came for one show, had some fun and never returned. Others stuck like glue and pestered me to make it a regular thing. So I did!

Unlike 1920s Berlin, The Old Time Radio Room is small and indeed portable. As a result, it has been possible for Klopstick to move to various sims. The show began in earnest in a room belonging to a friend and radio show enthusiast before being moved to another, similar, room in its current location. "One lesson I'd learned was not to get over-ambitious," Klopstick said, "so I kept it small and highly affordable [...] I'd seen too many other vintage places, gorgeous places, go bust because the upkeep was too expensive." While he initially attempted to ensure historical accuracy by requiring visitors to wear period-appropriate clothing and attend in human form in order to listen in the room (those with unrealistic avatars were provided with a space on the roof), he quickly gave up. "Some people got very militant about their avatars and clothing," he said, adding that controlling clothing was too stressful. The Old Time Radio Room no longer attempts to invoke historical truth. Instead, Klopstick provides a comfortable and familiar sense of "pastness" in which the very real historical artefacts he presents, his radio programmes, can be enjoyed.

Despite this limitation Klopstick aims to create an environment in which the radio shows he airs feel appropriate. To this end he has even included old photographs of his own parents in the décor. "My parents would be mortified to know they are immortalised in a virtual world," he said, adding "Dad might have been okay with it. Mom would have been creeped out, I think. I tried to explain the idea of SL to her years ago, but she just laughed hysterically and the shields went up." With the inclusion of these photographs, and of old-fashioned prim furniture whose creators "are long gone," Klopstick has created a multilayered space which speaks to his own family history and to SL's history just as it speaks to the American entertainment history which is at its core.

The three themes of this chapter—nostalgia for home, nostalgia for SL's own history, and time travel—provide some understanding of the many and varied ways in which residents are able, in this mature virtual world, to reflect upon, revisit, and reimagine the past. Lorelai and Isabelle, whose stories begin this chapter, demonstrate the extent to which class impacts both what is revisited and how this is done within the virtual world. Equally importantly, however, their narratives suggest that SL can be a space in which lost family memories can be recaptured and shared. Lorelai's recreation of her childhood home was constructed from memory with the aid of her mother. As such it is a creation borne both from the historical reality of her childhood home and her own creative and interpretive work in merging her memories with those of her mother. In Isabelle's case there was not an attempt to create a close to identical space to one inhabited in youth—instead, she sought, through creating camping grounds and hiking tracks alongside reconstructions of her mother's former holiday homes, to recreate the sense of such spaces and to provide a place in which the familial bonds of her memory could be reconstructed. In both of these cases, the mother-daughter bond was reconstituted and strengthened through acts of nostalgic recreation.

Lorelai's story reminded us in an oblique, yet resonate way, of Alejandro Amenabar's film *The Others* (2001). In this film an old house is inhabited by a mother and her young children who hear the sounds of other human presences and are afraid it is haunted by ghosts. The frightened, searching point of view of the mother in the film wants to discover the source of these disturbances. We can read later on in the film these disturbances—the apparent noises—as a form of psychical awakening. Through the search to find the source of the noisy disturbances, the film leads the viewer to believe that this family are indeed living in a haunted house. But this point of view takes a turn, and falls away, in the discovery of a family photograph album dedicated to documenting the images of deceased, former family members living in the house. In that moment we, the film viewers, realise that it is the family that we believed were the "alive" living occupants of the house who are in fact its real ghosts. The dead are represented in their deadness in the photograph album. The dead mother upon encountering the image of her own death and that of her children through the photographs (photographs are already emblems and objects of death as Barthes writes) comes to this shocking recognition and reversal of identity. The disturbance and the noise are the mechanism through which they (and we the film viewer) waken to their death, and the family wake up, paradoxically, to the recognition that they are the dead. As the true ghosts of haunting, it becomes their duty, then, to take their leave and return the house to the truly living.

Neither Lorelai nor her mother lives in the real-life family home reconstructed on the SL plot of virtual land. The home was packed away sometime after Lorelai showed it to her mother, and it now lives amongst Lorelai's inventory of property as one of her creative builds. At the time of the interview, there were no plans to bring it back into this virtual reality. MargieG actually asked Lorelai in the interview if she would be willing to "rezz" the family home again on her plot of land so that she could see and visit it. She didn't seem particularly keen to do this, and after MargieG asked her, she lost further contact. MargieG reflects:

> I wonder now, as I return to this interview after quite sometime of realising just how interesting and unexpected it was, what I was really asking of her. It is only now that I am working with this interview text in a concentrated, thoughtful way (I hope) that I have come to an understanding of the story as a story about the work of mourning. The reconstructed family home is a very personal 3D object of profound emotional attachment, embedded within close relationships. To "rezz" the object back to life for the purposes of my interest after being "packed away" (Lorlai's phrase) is not a simple act by any means.

Lorelai and her mother are not engaged in living a haunted house mode of nostalgia with a melancholic attachment to their real-life family home. Melancholia represents the failure or inability to go through mourning, and the lost object (often loved and hated as Freud argues) remains psychically invested to the point that it can be all consuming. This is certainly not the story of Lorelai and her mother. On the contrary, SL provided a place in which to recreate the missed, lost object of family memory and memories. As part of the work of mourning, the reconstructed virtual home has served its purpose—it returned in order for it to be ritually enacted as *here* because it is *gone*. This is a fundamental turning point of all mourning—that loss is recognised as lost.

CHAPTER 7

Conclusion

Today, the presence of digital technologies in our lives is taken for granted. Our homes are increasingly digitised. Our fridges can connect to the internet and remind us to buy more milk. We have personal robots in our homes, and we can command them to vacuum our floors while we ourselves are at work. Our personal communications are increasingly digital. As a result, digital technologies are necessarily formative in our identity. The internet has become like electricity—ever-present, part of the fabric of our lives, and only noticed when it ceases to operate correctly. These realities seem so very natural to us that it is at times difficult to remember just how new digital cultures really are. In 1995 Sherry Turkle wrote that:

> At one level, the computer is a tool. It helps us write, keep track of our accounts, and communicate with others. Beyond this, the computer offers us both new models of mind and a new medium on which to project our ideas and fantasies. Most recently, the computer has become even more than tool and mirror: We are able to step through the looking glass. We are learning to live in virtual worlds. We may find ourselves along as we navigate virtual oceans, unravel virtual mysteries, and engineer virtual skyscrapers. But increasingly, when we step through the looking glass, other people are there as well.[1]

[1] Sherry Turkle, *Life on the Screen: Identity in the Age of the Internet* (New York: Simon & Schuster, 1995), 9.

M. Gibson, C. Carden, *Living and Dying in a Virtual World*,
Palgrave Macmillan Memory Studies,
https://doi.org/10.1007/978-3-319-76099-5_7

SL was created eight years after Turkle's words were published. The very fact that we can now look upon a virtual world—a space in which we can step through the looking glass and interact with the other—and dismiss it as out of date is extraordinary. It speaks to an immense change which has occurred within living memory. We now live in an age in which digital obsolescence is taken for granted as part of our future. This has an impact on futures of loss, grief, and nostalgia. As authors, we came to the study of SL with very different generational understandings of the internet. Margaret has witnessed and researched the growing ubiquity of the internet with respect to cultures of mourning. She remembers a time before computers and mobile phones were ubiquitous and part of public cultures of mourning. For Clarissa, computers have always been part of life. She played online video games such as Neopets, while a student at primary school and as a teenager, many of her closest friendships were formed and maintained online. We both remember a time when the internet was expensive, accessed through telephone cables, and therefore limited. Today we live and work in an environment in which the temporary loss of online connectivity would be at best a major inconvenience and at worst a catastrophe. SL as a mature virtual world is marked by associations and realities of middle-aged participants. Our technologies age us. They place our biographies in time. They are also resources for the politics of ageism wherein a place like SL can be overwhelmingly dismissed in part because of the age of its participants. It is therefore inherently imbedded in the ageism that digital cultures can produce.

Such rapid technological change has necessarily been associated with corresponding social changes. However, the experiences of our research participants demonstrate that these social changes, as they relate to recognition of grief and loss, have been insufficient. The grief of residents who have lost loved ones online has largely been disenfranchised in their offline lives. Just as users of social media have responded creatively and intuitively to the deaths of loved ones,[2] so too have SL residents worked within the boundaries of their own virtual world to alternatively replicate and reimagine offline rituals of mourning.

The disenfranchisement of grief within this context is associated not only with the digital nature of the environment but also with its unique

[2] B. Carroll and K. Landry, "Logging On and Letting Out: Using Online Social Networks to Grieve and to Mourn," *Bulletin of Science, Technology & Society* 30, no. 5 (October 1, 2010): 341–49, https://doi.org/10.1177/0270467610380006.

nature. SL was one of a group of virtual worlds which came online in the early 2000s. Not all have survived. The Sims Online, later EA Online, is a notable example of a world which, despite being loved by its residents, did not make it. Of those that have continued, some, like World of Warcraft, are game-focused. The purpose of their existence, and for the continued interaction of users, is apparently self-evident. Second Life provides no such explanation for its own continuation. It continues to exist because it remains in use—but the reasons residents choose to live in SL may be as numerous as residents themselves.

Due to its age, SL, while no longer cutting-edge technology, is still a very new type of entity. Mature virtual worlds have not and could not have existed at any other moment in history. Never before has it been possible for residents to have engaged so extensively and for such long periods of time in a single digital environment. Our ideas of what constitute meaningful relationships, and the way in which these relationships should be remembered, have simply failed to live up to the rate of change. While there is a great deal of ubiquity to memorialisation online, it is easy to forget that there are still people who are surprised by this phenomenon and are not willing or comfortable participants.

Existing media discourses pathologise long-term engagement with virtual worlds such as SL. If SL is inherently and necessarily secondary, it can be redefined as a distraction, a space in which individuals unreasonably and unfairly spend time which could be more usefully employed elsewhere. This perspective has informed the salacious media coverage which accompanied SL's early years and, arguably, has contributed to an almost complete refusal on the part of major media sources to engage with SL in more recent years. There are, of course, exceptions, such as *The Atlantic*'s 2017 article "The Digital Ruins of a Forgotten Future."[3] As the name implies, however, this article, while sensitive and extensive, ultimately positions SL as something that is not quite comprehensible. There is almost a sense of confusion that this virtual world, which is no longer new and which appears not to have lived up to its initial promise, has stubbornly refused to die.

However, this book has demonstrated that SL continues to be a space in which significant and valuable lives are lived. The distinction between

[3] Leslie Jamison, "The Digital Ruins of a Forgotten Future," *The Atlantic*, December 2017, https://www.theatlantic.com/magazine/archive/2017/12/second-life-leslie-jamison/544149/.

"real" and "virtual" lives reflects a biological fact. Avatars cannot age, or die, or experience the sensation of touch. Avatar life cannot exist independently of physical embodied life. The avatar is in this sense secondary—its death cannot end the existence of the human operator, even though the opposite is true. This purely pragmatic view of firstness and secondness not only obscures the lived reality of second lives, it also speaks against a discourse which holds that the "true self" exists independent of the circumstances of our physical lives. This discourse has been powerful in shaping our understandings of the relationship between computers and mortality. Computers can only be understood as offering a potential salve for mortality if the "true" self can exist outside of the physical body. This understanding of the "true" self is also prevalent in the perspectives of SL residents, who see SL as a place in which they are freed from the constraints of their embodied lives and can finally live "truly."

There are of course significant philosophical questions associated with the body/mind split and the reality of the disembodied "true" self. However, the fact that this discourse appears to be able to coexist with a pathologising view of virtual world residents suggests a limited psychological and medicalised conception of reality and selfhood. Grief on social media may be new, but it can be accepted and comprehended in part because social media profiles are generally associated with one's "true" self. Facebook profiles usually feature a photograph of the user and information such as their gender, age, and location. Connections on Facebook are often, although not always, primarily people one knows offline. In SL, the anchor of the "real" is not as present and is less relevant.

We posit that the idea of "digital flesh" helps us to theoretically move past the distinction between the first and second lives. "Digital flesh" is developed through continued engagement and investments of time in the virtual world. Where time spent online has been inflected with major and life-defining experiences, the distinction between physical and digital cannot retain its moral meaning. Residents speak of the need to remember the reality and significance of the person "behind the screen," but our research shows that it is equally the person "within" the screen, or the person known through the screen, which carries moral weight. Where a loss occurs—a person is known to have died offline or even simply ceases to sign into SL—moral weight becomes impossible to ignore. In this sense it is through loss that the reality of the digital flesh becomes realised.

The digital flesh of the other can be encountered and valued through the screen. It can be loved and grieved in and of itself. However, such lives are necessarily tethered to mortal, physical lives. It is not necessary for a resident to know the facts of that physical life to mourn and care for their virtual loved one. However, the very fact that the other encountered online is necessarily a mortal other matters.

The hierarchies and values of meaning in which firstness and secondness are comprehensible as ways of ordering relationships are delicate and can be unravelled. The process of engaging in SL in an extended way, developing one's own digital flesh, contributes to this unravelling. So too do the ways in which the "real" becomes part of the "virtual," such as through the construction of sentimental objects that mimic lost or remembered physical objects. The broad scope for creation offered by SL means that, at times, nostalgia for one's own history can be engaged in more meaningfully and creatively online than offline. The longing to recuperate our past speaks to a deeply human need. SL both assuages this need and provides a vehicle through which it can be expressed. It allows residents to accept what is true for us all—that we do long for people and things that have passed.

The moral reality of SL has been solidified by the duration of its existence. In a sense SL is haunted by the ghosts of residents who are no longer present. Their imprint can be found in the items they created which continue to circulate. It is evident in the sims they frequented and in the markers and memorials constructed by those who are left behind. Outside of cemeteries, the presence of the dead is invisible to new residents or to those who are insufficiently engaged with the communities that are haunted. Loss therefore creates communities of knowers and people who do not or cannot know.

In an important sense, the spatiality of SL and the variety of means through which individuals are able to leave their marks on the spaces of SL create the means through which the spectres of the dead are able to haunt the living. This is in a sense no different to offline spaces which are necessarily haunted and marked by the lives of those who have been there before. However, the nature of SL makes extreme changes in environments continuous and expected. Residents can create or contribute to spaces, but this does not render them permanent. Thus significant places of memory can cease to exist quite suddenly. In fact, their continued existence is often contingent upon circumstances outside of the control of the residents to whom they matter the most. It takes a very specific set of circumstances for a resident to be able to ensure the continued existence of the spaces that matter to them and upon which their biographies are marked. The loss of an entire neighbourhood is not something which can occur overnight in the physical world. In SL it can happen without warning if the owner of a sim suddenly decides to delete their creation or ceases to pay their land usage fees. Residents who have been engaged with SL for a long period of time often have a nostalgic connection to places and things which have disappeared. This problem is exacerbated by the fact that the creations of residents continue to exist and be accessible in-world when they themselves are offline, meaning that the owner of a sim may never have encountered the people to whom it is significant.

This tenuous connection to significant objects and spaces is exacerbated by rumours of SL's impending death. Linden Lab has been spruiking a new virtual reality project, Project Sansar, for a few years. It has gained support from prominent SL residents who have been invited to create spaces and objects within this new environment. It has, however, led to real fears among members of the SL population who suspect that SL will eventually be shut down. If this were to occur, it would follow a string of other virtual worlds—notably including The Sims Online—which have been destroyed after becoming unprofitable. This is a danger inherent in investing heavily in a virtual world, one which likely contributes to the ideas of firstness and secondness which remain an important part of the language of residents. However, residents do not act with a constant awareness of or fear of the possibility of SL's impending death. The longevity of this virtual world has created a situation in which its life can be projected into the future—it has become a taken-for-granted part of individual biographies which is not understood as facing an imminent end unless residents stop to consider this as a possibility. It is this taken-for-grantedness, this association with individual memory and biography, which characterises SL as a mature virtual world.

Yet SL does not function independently or outside of the physical world. Its history is its own, but it is interwoven with the history of the world offline in both an individual and collective sense. There are spaces in which a resident is transported to an imagined version of a time and place in the history of Europe or the USA. In this book we have discussed 1920s Berlin, but there are also historical representations of Chicago, Texas, Rome, London, and others. In these locations the work of heritage associated with the upkeep of memories and physical places or objects is overtaken by a new kind of heritage work which is rooted in experience and emotion. The heritage sites one encounters in these spaces are not carefully preserved and contextualised in relation to a history which encompasses that which followed their moment of prominence. Instead, they are spaces in which one can live history devoid of context. In a way this allows for a more accurate understanding of individual biography in relation to historical metanarratives—these spaces provide one with a sense that those residing within them do not know what comes next—theirs is an unknown and unseeable future. Yet the users of the avatars do indeed know the future and are thus in a situation in which a future is known but not known, full of possibilities and yet constrained.

Second Life is a haunted virtual world with various forms of spectrality around lost and deceased lives, the persistence of memory, and the persistence of grievability, but it is also a world that regenerates itself. There are always new projects on the horizon. The extent to which these projects are likely to materialise in SL itself is open to question. The future of this world cannot be assured any more than could the futures of those virtual worlds that have gone before. What is certain, however, is that those residents who have developed important networks of relatedness and who have engaged in the acts of memory we detail in this book will find ways to maintain those networks and those memories.

Computers promised us immortality. They are traditionally associated with ideals of logic, rationality, and a lack of emotion. What they have given us instead is a new means through which we can perform that most human of actions—connecting to one another. As our friendships, our romantic partnerships, and our working relationships move increasingly online, we must take seriously the possibilities and threats opened up by increasingly digital lifestyles. We can meet people with whom our paths would never physically cross. We can share our lives with intimate others who are on the other side of the globe and yet simultaneously present within our own living rooms. These connections may broaden our horizons and change our lives for the better. But they also open us up to that other, deeply human, experience: loss. How we will recognise that loss, and the moral status we accord to it, is key question for the future.

Index

A
Avatar
 appearance, 9, 54, 56, 79, 137
 gender, 14

C
Class, 21, 30, 38, 63, 65, 132, 133, 141
Commemorative culture
 cemetery, 20, 85, 93
 grave, 79, 87, 93, 95–97
 memorial, 83, 90, 94, 103

D
Death
 grief, 17, 21
 loss, 25, 40, 81, 84, 99, 100
 mourning, vii, ix, 80, 81, 84, 87, 100
Digital flesh, 3, 5, 28, 33–36, 49, 53, 60, 62, 70, 95, 109, 114, 148, 149
 disappearance, 128
 search for missing loved ones, 48
Disenfranchised grief, 11, 26
 Doka, 11

F
Families
 adoption, 24, 41, 42, 64
 babies, 24, 41, 64, 69, 92
 blended families, 19, 23–49, 64
 children, 19, 27, 40–42, 44, 45, 49, 69, 118
 constructed families, 38, 44
 digital kinship, 19, 23, 25, 96
 pregnancy, 64, 118
 siblings, 24, 25, 38, 39, 49

G
Grievable lives, 51–77
 Butler, 103

M. Gibson, C. Carden, *Living and Dying in a Virtual World*,
Palgrave Macmillan Memory Studies,
https://doi.org/10.1007/978-3-319-76099-5

H

History
  1920s Berlin, 21, 137–138, 150
  play, 138
  truth, 113, 141

L

LGBTIQ, 84
  gay, 84, 85

M

Memory, vii–ix, 3, 5, 8–10, 17, 18, 20, 21, 23, 26, 27, 52, 64, 80, 83–85, 92, 93, 96, 99, 101–103, 105, 108, 110–118, 124, 127, 129–135, 141–143, 146, 149–151
  haunting, 149

N

Nostalgia, ix, 8, 21, 93, 127–143, 146, 149
  home, 21, 118, 130–133, 141, 143

P

Photographs, 31, 35, 47, 69, 76, 92, 99, 105, 109, 111, 113–115, 121, 129, 134, 141, 142, 148

R

Reality
  real lives, 59–70, 94
  RL, 34
  touchstone of the real, 35
Relationships
  friendship, 24, 30, 35, 38, 39, 96, 108, 151
  love, 24, 26, 34, 35, 37, 46, 98
  romantic relationships, 11, 23, 27, 29, 30, 32–35, 46, 99
Replication, 48, 118
Rituals, viii, 12, 26, 48, 49, 73, 80, 83, 84, 94, 101, 103, 146

S

Secrets, 37
Sentimental objects, 107–125, 149
  animals (cats, dogs), 118, 121, 122

T

Time travel, 21, 131, 135–143

V

Virtual worlds, vii, viii, 3–8, 10, 11, 13, 16, 17, 19–21, 26, 28, 29, 36, 41, 45, 49, 53, 54, 58–60, 66, 70, 71, 77, 85, 86, 100, 108, 109, 112, 117, 120, 125, 129, 133, 135, 137, 138, 141, 145–148, 150, 151
  mature virtual world, vii, 10, 21, 141, 146, 147, 150

The manufacturer's authorised representative in the EU is Springer Nature Customer Service Centre GmbH, Europaplatz 3, 69115 Heidelberg, Germany. If you have any concerns regarding our products, please contact ProductSafety@springernature.com

Printed and bound by CPI Group (UK) Ltd, Croydon, CR0 4YY
05/10/2026
02228161-0002